MW01105048

Approaching
DAWN

NANCY MORRISON

 **FriesenPress**

Suite 300 - 990 Fort St
Victoria, BC, Canada, V8V 3K2
www.friesenpress.com

ISBN
978-1-4602-6435-5 (Hardcover)
978-1-4602-6436-2 (Paperback)
978-1-4602-6437-9 (eBook)

1. *History, Native American*

Distributed to the trade by The Ingram Book Company

CONTENTS

ACKNOWLEDGEMENT

I gratefully acknowledge the support of my family and friends who have encouraged me through the writing of this book and throughout my life. You are too numerous to mention and too important to be forgotten. I will remember you always.

I also acknowledge the help of my special friends from Making Kenora Home. Nan Normand patiently transcribed my words while Selen Alpay generously facilitated the publication of this book to ensure that my story can be shared long after I have gone.

DEDICATION

TO MY FAMILY

I wish to dedicate my story to the memory of my beloved husband, Victor. I thank him for his endless love, support and encouragement. Although I miss him, I know we will meet again in the Spirit World.

I thank my parents for my existence and especially appreciated the comfort and constant caring by my *nindede*, Norman. The memory of his reassuring hugs is dear to me.

I thank the Creator for the gift of my children. They have been my joy. *Miigwech* to both of them for the love they have shown me.

Many, many moons have passed since the Great Spirit called my *nookum*, Josephine, to rest. Your teachings have stayed with me through the years and lead me into a future very different from the life you lived. Your teaching will be carried beyond my time as sacred wisdom is relayed to the next generation.

Andy, Caroline and Randy White—have always come when called to assist me with the Healing Workshops and Sharing Circles. Your willingness to squeeze in yet another activity on my request is evidence of the respectfulness with which you walk the Earth.

TO MY FRIENDS

Dr. Allen M. Torrie supported us in bringing the wisdom of the Elders forward. He and his wife shared many memorable times with us through the Mishomis/Nookomis project. It was meant to be a four-year project but its success pulled it forward fourteen years. Dr. Torrie worked respectfully beside us, encouraging us to bring healing to our people. It was an honour to be part of the project team. I remain grateful for Dr. Torrie's invitation to join in this important work. I am also appreciative of the support of my colleagues during this work.

My work on the While People Sleep project was supported by the commitment of Cuyler Cotton, who helped me to search out the homeless. Through snowdrifts and back alleys, he walked with me to talk with my people. After all these years, his commitment is still honoured by me. I wish to say *"Kitche Miigwech"* to the man I call my friend.

The staff of the Fellowship Centre have always encouraged and supported me in helping my people. Much was accomplished because of these individuals. I give a special thank you to Rev. Steve Robinson and Rev. Henry Hildebrandt whose leadership served the most marginalized of our community.

Judy Da Silva and her drum group have freed the voice of the women. I thank them for raising up their drums and supporting our women.

Mike Aiken supported me in attending many of the residential school healing workshops throughout our region. This allowed me to participate further than my feet could take me. *Miigwech*.

TO MY PEOPLE

Finally, I dedicate this book to the honour of all survivors of residential school trauma. My story is only one of many and each deserves to be told. Each deserves to be understood. Each deserves to be respected. I pray for their healing and I pray for the healing of our nations.

I have shared my story so those who come after me can know of the past and go into the future with courage of our grandmothers and grandfathers. I know my people will continue to rise and will prosper in the coming times.

HOPE

With a single beat, the drum falls into silence. The Elder moves forward into the circle, head bowed in thought. The diminutive figure raises the eagle feather. Those in the room edge forward. The sharing is about to begin.

"When I was very young, my grandmother taught me the ways of our people. When I went to residential school, I was taught to be ashamed—ashamed of my people and ashamed of our ways. I was beaten when I spoke of my grandmother's teachings. I was punished when I spoke our language. I tried to be White like the Jesus on the wall. It was a bad time and trying to walk on someone else's path just gets you lost."

Her story voice rolls out, increasing in strength as the words flow. Many in the audience identify with her pain. They also were in residential school. Others have heard the stories from their parents and grandparents. The impact of the colonial system traumatized generation after generation—an entire culture sharing one pain.

"I was lost. I had a home and a husband to love me but the pain of the past pulled me into the bottle. I turned my back on those who loved me because nothing could numb me like liquor. I lived on the streets because I was ashamed."

Tears trail down her softly weathered cheeks. She wipes them away with the back of her hand and then pauses to look at them shimmering against her dark skin.

1

"When I was at residential school we were told never to cry. I got caught crying once. I was a little child and I missed my family. I cried out of loneliness. The punishment for being a crybaby was to have to kneel in front of the other students with cut onions placed under your eyes. I knelt there feeling the burning in my eyes and the public humiliation of the punishment. I didn't get caught crying again."

She falls silent, taking measured breaths. Then, gathering her resolve, she begins again.

"I am telling you to cry for your pain. My grandmother taught me that tears wash pain away. You need to cry to begin healing."

Around the room, others bow their heads to quietly wipe away their own tears. It is pain shared—healing beginning.

"My grandmother also taught me that there is no such thing as hopelessness in life. There is an end to hope only when you are put into the ground. Somehow hope managed to find a way to ease into my life and it came in the form of a plea—*wiijiniin* (help me)."

Her message is a call to hopefulness, and her people hold tightly to her words.

"When I was a street person, there was pain. But, the worst for me, was when I heard that my own brother said that I was hopeless. He had given up on me. Later, when my life had changed, I told him how much that had hurt—and how that went against our grandmother's teaching. He explained to me that he has said it out of his own pain. His pain was caused by his inability to help me. He tried to push away the pain of his caring by giving up on me. He didn't know what else to do.

"There was nothing that he could do. I had to live it until the time came for change. I was tough, but for a woman on the streets there's always someone bigger, meaner, and tougher. There was one thing that I knew for sure—there would always be hope for as long as I lived. There was one thing I felt for sure—there was something unseen supporting me in surviving the streets. I didn't know what it was but I did know that I was brought safely out of too many dangerous situations for it to be a coincidence. I didn't understand it, but I felt it. Years later I read a poem called 'Footprints'. It was about how we are carried through our troubled times by God. Now I say miigwech to the Creator every day, and every night, before I sleep.

"The Creator gave me a good man. I will always be grateful for my husband's patience. No matter what I did, he said that my home would be waiting for me. Time, and time again, he held out his hand without judgment. One thing a drunk can never say is never. The pull is always there. I tried and fell, and tried and fell. I couldn't do it on my own, and I'm telling you, none of you can do it on your own. You can call on God or Jesus or Allah or the Creator. It is all about the strength of a greater being. It is about believing in something bigger than you.

"It changed for me when I realized that. I knew I couldn't do it. I knew the love of my family wasn't enough. I finally said, quite simply, I need help and put it into the Creator's hands. When I returned to my husband something was different. My sister-in-law looked at me and said, 'You've changed. There is something I see in your eyes that reassures me that you won't drink again.' Of course, I reminded her to never say never to a drunk, but she was right. Something was different this time."

Her eyes still shine with resolve forty years later. Her husband is gone now. Her voice chokes as she shares the love between them during her years of sobriety.

"One day I noticed that my husband was staring at me so I asked him about it. He said to me, 'I'm not really staring at you but at what you have become. You're a walking miracle.'"

She wipes another tear sliding down her cheek and reminds everyone again tears are for healing.

"I was at home with the husband I loved but I felt pulled back to the streets. It was a different pull this time. Because of my experiences, I knew what they were feeling. I knew how crucial hope was in their lives. My husband told me to go. He trusted me. He supported the work that I felt compelled to do."

She smiles wistfully and continues.

"It's been many years and I have worked on many projects. I have received honours that I didn't want, and recognition that I didn't need. What I have to say to you is this: As long as you live there is hope."

As she moves through the throng, the soft tones of the *Anishinaabe,* call out to her. Hands reach toward the frail figure, and she pulls them closer, wrapping them in the warmth of her wisdom.

As long as you live there is hope.

MY BEGINNING

The process of writing my story is hard for me. Our people have an oral tradition. I prefer to speak face to face, heart to heart. But my speaking is ending, so I have committed to putting my words onto paper for those who live after me.

I have lived a long time. Much of my life was not happy, but I need to share what I know, because for many of my people, the story of my life is also the story of their lives. Our stories were taken from us in the silence that supported the residential school system. In that silence, our pain has been trapped in each of us, echoing through each generation. The time has come to tell our stories, shed our tears—and go forward.

At residential school, I was told that my story is that I was born on January 25, 1929, near the town of Kenora, Ontario. That story is marked with dates and places that do not have meaning for our people. That is not how my people tell their stories. It is our history that creates each of us—not a spot on a map, nor a date on the calendar. Most of the birth information given to us at residential school was not even accurate. Indian agents often guessed at dates and places. Once it was written down, we were told it was the truth.

For the *Anishinaabe*, the history of our families and clans define us. My *nimaamaa* (mother) was Ethel Cheena. She was from *Iskatewizaagegan* (Shoal Lake). My *nindede* (father) was Norman Kelly. He was assigned to the Sabaskong First Nation, but he was really from *Mishkosiminiziibiing* near Morson. The Indian agents told us where we belonged, and through their misunderstandings, many of our families ended up relocated away from their people. My *nookum* (grandmother) spent her life in *Wauzhushk Onigum* (Rat Portage). Her name was Josephine Skead. Her husband was a respected medicine man. My *doodem* is *Bizhiw* (Lynx Clan). We are responsible for defending and healing our people.

I was a very sick baby. My *nindede* and *nimaammaa* could do no more for me. In desperation, they took me to a traditional healer. He told them I would live a long time and told my parents a prophecy. This is when I was given my spiritual name—*Pay Comikeezhegook* (Approaching Dawn). My every day name was Nancy.

I recovered from my illness. It was not I who died too early, but my *nimaamaa*. I was three years old when she passed. Years later I told my *nookum* of a disturbing dream I had. I was being held in someone's arms and was looking down at something wrapped in a beige cloth with red dots. I could remember no more, except for an overwhelming feeling of loss. My *nookum* sat quietly and did not answer me for a while. When she finally spoke she took my hand in hers and started talking.

"*Noozhesans* (grandchild)," she said, "I am going to tell you a very sad story now that you are old enough to understand. It is hard for me to answer you. You were three years old when your *nimaamaa* passed away. You were there at her funeral. What you describe was not a dream."

I have since located where my *nimaamaa* was buried. It is in a spot south of where the residential school was. After all these years, I'm still very grateful to my *nookum* for showing me where both my parents are now at rest.

It is the tradition of the *Anishinaabe* when a parent dies the grandparent will take care of the children. This is how we took care of our own. There was no need for Children's Aid Societies back then because we understood responsibility. When my *nimaamaa* died, I was the only child not already in residential school. My *nindede* had to return to work, so my *nookomis* (grandmother) took care of me. Her house was poor, but we had what we needed, and there was love. She lived in a single-room log cabin. Like all the reserve houses there was no plumbing or electricity; the wood stove provided heat and cooking. When it was hot, we cooked outside.

I had an older brother, three sisters, and uncles who were attending another residential school. I remember meeting them only on summer holidays, so my siblings were practically strangers to me. By the time I was old enough to relate to them there was only one sister left living.

"Where are the other two?" I asked *nookum*. "Where are my sisters?"

Her answer was that they died on two separate occasions due to beatings. When I asked her who did it, she didn't answer. She began crying. I didn't want her to hurt anymore so I didn't ask more questions. Now I always wonder where they are buried.

According to *nookum*, this is what happened next in our lives. She and I were alone at her home at Wauzhushk Onigum. There was a knock at the door. When she opened the door she saw three men—an Indian Agent, a Mountie, and an Indian, who was acting as the interpreter. He explained they were there to get me. I would be taken to a place where I would be looked after better than the way we were living.

She tried to tell them it was her responsibility to look after me. They would not listen so she wrapped her arms around me to hold me close to her. The Mountie pulled me away from her. Because I was just a child I did not understand what was happening. I remember being fascinated by those shiny buttons on the Mountie's jacket. I kept looking at those buttons while the adults spoke. The interpreter told her I would not be taken far, so *nookum* let me go. She was afraid of the men, but she followed so she would know where I was being taken. I was only three years old.

EARLY SCHOOL YEARS

Nookum tried to watch over me at the residential school. She would walk over to check on me, and ask how I was being treated. She knew what went on at the school. I can remember sitting in her lap, and being comforted with her presence. When she had to leave I would hold on to her tightly. One of the nuns would have to pull me away. I would cry and struggle, so the nun would hit me to make me stop my fussing. This is the first abuse I remember.

Later, I asked *nookum* her why I was in a different school than my brother and sisters. They were at the Presbyterian school and I was sent to the Roman Catholic school. Her answer was that she was glad I was placed there. It was close enough she could walk to see me. The residential school I attended was located near to where she had lived all her life at Wauzhushk Onigum. My older siblings had gone to the other residential school, which was a long ways to walk to.

I don't remember too much of the first years I spent at the residential school. I kept everybody awake by crying so much. The older girls were ordered to keep me quiet, and they tried. Usually I would end up in bed with one of them, but then the Sister would tell me I had to sleep in my own bed. After going back to my own bed, I would cry again, and it would go on and on.

Finally the Sister got fed up with my crying. She grabbed me and pushed me into the middle of the playroom. I remember the girls backing away from us. I was forced to kneel down. Cut onions were placed over my eyes and a blindfold held them tightly against my face. The fumes burnt fiercely. The Sister told the girls that if they ever cried for nothing, like babies, they would get the same treatment.

I don't know how long I had to kneel there. My knees ached. My eyes stung. Finally, the Sister tapped me on the head with her wooden stick. I was ordered to pray for myself so I could quit crying. I never cried in front of a nun again.

When I was about four years old, I remember wetting my bed. The Sister pulled my sheet and blanket away from me. She grabbed me by my hair and shoved my face into the wet spot. Then she hit me with her stick.

The nun was not finished with me yet. She yanked me toward the bathroom where I was thrown in a tub of very hot water. I remember screaming and being very frightened. But it didn't stop me from wetting the bed. So, I kept getting the same treatment over and over again, as did other girls. I still don't understand how scalding us would keep us from peeing during the night.

There was a grotto on the hillside near the girl's playground that sheltered the statue there of the Blessed Virgin. The Sister explained to us, that in order to be good little girls, we should get down on our knees to pray. At recess time, the Sister called out our names, and we were ordered to go there to spend time in prayer. It must have been very important to her, because if we didn't do as she said we would get punished. There were always two girls on vigil, praying while the others played. We all had turns doing prayer duty. The Sister dutifully punished any of us who did not perform our prayers properly.

We all had to wear the same clothing. The clothes were made by the students under direction of the nuns in the sewing room. There were weekday clothes and Sunday clothes. Our arms and legs had to be covered at all times. They said they were teaching us to be ladies, instead of dirty squaws. Our hands had to be folded together in front of us when we weren't working. Our legs had to always be together at the knees when we were seated. Breaking the "lady rules" meant we were hit with sticks and called names. We didn't even know what the names meant, but we knew to follow the strange rules to avoid the blows.

When I was about six, classes started. Classes were for only two or three hours a day. The actual training that went on in the schools was primarily directed towards maintaining the institutions. The learning was training for domestic service. The students were the free labour that fuelled the operation. Girls would be cleaning, sewing, cooking, and doing the laundry for the entire school. Boys would be doing the heavier work—cutting wood to keep the facility heated, building and repairing, planting crops, tending to the animals, and yard work. This work went on day after day.

It was the responsibility of the big girls to show us what to do. At first I was taught to dust, and then to scrub and polish floors until they shined. As I got older, I learned to help in the kitchen and to sew. The Sisters would check each piece of work we did. If it wasn't done right, we were punished. Punishment was always there—hanging heavy over us.

Residential school was training to serve the Whites. In school, we served the principal, priest, and nuns. We grew their crops, cleaned their quarters, washed their clothes, and prepared their food. That was our role. We learned to follow orders without question, because to displease our superiors resulted in painful consequences. As servants, we were taught to put their needs ahead of our own. By becoming servants we lost our ability to think for ourselves and to lead our own people. Whites were the leaders, and we weren't to challenge that rule. Not only did we lose our leadership, but also we lost our sense of family—along with our culture. Because we were separated from our parents, we did not learn how to parent through traditional example. Because we became disconnected from the circle of life, we lost what was most precious—how to live in a family and how to live in a community.

RELIGION

Reading, writing and arithmetic was just preparation for religion class. The school existed to make us obedient—and Catholic. I didn't do well at either.

I remember the priest coming into the classroom to teach us. A priest was special, so we had to be extra careful to avoid punishment. The teacher passed out pencils and pieces of paper to each of us to follow along with what the priest was trying to teach us. We all had our names printed on the paper, so the teacher would know who was really paying attention—and who wasn't. I struggled to get the answers right, but no matter how hard I tried I was wrong. The teacher would punch my ears, or hit me elsewhere, for getting religion wrong. We were always reminded we must try harder to learn what we were taught. If we failed we did not deserve to be baptized. We weren't sure what that was but it was obviously important.

Just in case we didn't know how important religion was, we were taught fear. The girls were taken down to the recreation room to watch a silent film. The movie showed a devil holding a big pitchfork pushing people into a fire called Hell. After that movie we all headed toward the dormitory, holding onto each other tightly for fear we might encounter something along the way in dark places. I remember praying so hard before I went to bed. One of us would wake up with a nightmare and we would run together into a heap of frightened girls. Then we would be in trouble for being out of bed.

Having learned the word "Hell", I wondered who went there? The Sister said people who did very bad deeds were called sinners, and they would stay in Hell forever. This frightened me terribly. People who acted well, and prayed all the time, went to Heaven and were happy forever. So that's where I wanted to go. But when?

I could not get that out of my mind. I was too afraid of the Sister to ask her when we would go to Heaven. I finally asked an older friend. The girl told me when someone dies they go to Heaven. She went on to say, "When I die, don't feel sad. Be happy because I will be in Heaven and no one will abuse me anymore." I still remember her words. Yet, I often wonder if this was her suicide wish? Was Heaven our escape from the abuse of residential school?

The Sister reminded us the day of our baptism was approaching soon. April was the month we were to be baptized. The names of those chosen to receive Holy Sacrament were called out. Our orders were to practice until our prayers were perfect. For me, it was very exciting, but there was a problem. The Sister would randomly test us. Being afraid of her, I would get nervous and forget the words. Forgetting our religious studies was very bad. It meant I deserved to be hit and called names.

We had to learn about confession in order to take Communion. The Sister showed us the confessional. It had a dim light inside and was divided in two parts by a screen. On one side, the priest would sit to hear our sins. On the other side, there was a place to kneel while we confessed our sins. Not understanding too much, but wanting to learn, I put my hand up to ask a question like the Sister taught us to do. I asked, "How do we all fit in there?" She must have thought I was being sarcastic. She came toward me with her stick. The girls around me scattered. The Sister hit me across my head, calling me stupid. I was thrown out of chapel and pushed roughly into the playroom next door. I know I tried to hide my tears so the Sister would not notice, but you couldn't hide anything from her. She noticed. She angrily pushed me toward the sink and scrubbed my eyes with soap and water as punishment for crying.

Saturday was the day we were scheduled to go to confession. We had to practice the ritual over and over again so we would do it right. Finally, it was my turn. I knew what the Sister wanted me to say. I still remember what I was to say:

Me: Bless me, Father, for I have sinned.

Priest: What sins have you done?

Me: Touching myself where I'm not supposed to be, lying, saying bad words, and thinking bad thoughts.

Priest: Are you really sorry?

Me: Yes.

He blessed me and told me to recite ten Hail Marys. When I left the confessional, the Sister must have already known what my penance would be. She ordered me to go kneel down at the front of the altar and to do what Father ordered. This became our weekly routine. That was how little girls were made into Catholics.

We had to be fitted in special clothes for our special day. A different sister, who worked in the sewing room, called a few girls at a time to try on some very pretty clothes and veils. The big girls helped us into the all-white outfits. There were even beautiful black patent shoes for us to wear. When all the girls were done we were told to stand together to wait.

Sister Superior entered. A feeling of fear came upon me. The only time I saw her was at the office to be punished. The regular sister would take me there because I had done something bad—like not getting into line fast enough, or whispering to another girl when we were to be silent. Sister Superior made the bigger punishment decisions. The daily slaps and name-calling wasn't considered real punishment. Sister Superior would decide if we were to be strapped or denied food. Most of the time I was ordered to get on my knees and pray in front of the girls, but there was always the fear there would be more punishment. When she entered the sewing room, I thought we would all be punished for some unknown deed. I was so scared.

Sister Superior spoke, and I was surprised. She told us she was very proud we were to be baptized on Easter Sunday. Each of us would receive a white rosary after baptism. She said we would come out of the chapel as pure as the angels. She wanted to make sure everything was done right, so we practiced again for her by walking to the chapel in a single file.

I believed I would become an angel with wings and a halo like the ones in the picture books. I wanted to be an angel like Sister Superior said we would be. I knew angels were perfect, so they wouldn't have to be punished.

On Easter, the Sister woke us up early and told us to run to the east-facing windows. It was our ritual to watch the sun come up on the day Jesus rose from the dead. It was our responsibility to pray.

After the ritual and prayer, the older girls, who had been assigned to be our godmothers, came in to help us into our fancy white clothes. Even they got to wear pretty dresses. We were then taken into the playroom where Sister Superior was waiting. She warned us to do everything right. Those of us who giggled in excitement were hit with her stick to teach us dignity.

Our signal to enter the chapel was when the organist began playing. Boys and girls started singing. We entered, and walked toward the altar, with our hands folded in prayer, holding our rosaries. As I passed the pews, I noticed there were parents in the sanctuary. I was so proud when I spotted my *nindede*, but my *nookum* was not there.

When the ceremony was over, we were told we could visit our parents later. The Sister told us to hurry and change our clothes, because we'd need them for our First Communion which would come after bapism. We changed our clothing as quickly as we could.

Once we were all dressed in our pink Sunday dresses, we were ordered to line up to go down for breakfast. There was a great surprise waiting for us. Our parents had been invited to join us for a special feast. Our usual breakfast was porridge, white bread spread with lard, and tea or milk. This feast consisted of one egg each, two pieces of ham, and toast! Best of all, we were told our parents could stay as long as they wanted. It was a brief taste of Heaven.

We were given enough food to keep our bodies growing. It was porridge and soup mostly. The food for the staff was different. We cooked and served roasts, vegetables, and desert. Each meal was a feast. The food smelled so good but it was not for us. The staff and priests were closer to Heaven, so their food was deserved, or so we thought. Perhaps that is why we were given that brief taste following our baptism and first communion—to encourage us to be better Christians.

After all of our exciting Easter activities, we went back to our regular routine. I went back to the classroom with the others for the morning, until it was time for lunch. After lunch, we did chores. When our work was done to the Sister's satisfaction, we were allowed to play outside until the older girls were done their class.

Nookum must have known the regular schedule. She would appear at the side of the playground after our chores were done. I would watch for her. It always seemed like such a long time between visits. I was always afraid she wouldn't be allowed to come. I knew the Sister didn't like her. She had told me in front of the girls I should be ashamed of my grandmother because she was an evil witch and a savage. There were other awful things she would say about my *nookum*. I was old enough to understand what was said, and it used to hurt me so much knowing there was nothing I could do about it. If I were to answer back I would have been beaten. The Sister couldn't stop *nookum* from coming to the edge of the property, but she could forbid me from seeing her.

After my baptism, *nookum* came for a visit. I went to sit down with her in our usual shady spot. I was so excited to show her my rosary. She asked me where I got it. I told her it was a gift from Sister Superior when I got baptized. It was a big surprise to *nookum*. She didn't seem to understand what baptism meant. I explained what I knew, but she didn't understand my explanation. For me it was about the white veils, black shiny shoes and the sparkling rosary. I think my father kept my baptism secret from my grandmother. He, and one of *nookum's* brothers, had also been baptized so they learned to keep secrets.

After this visit, *nookum* never asked or spoke about ceremonies at the residential school again. She told me she would not come again for a long time. By then I was getting used to being in school, and was settled in the day-to-day activities, but learning she would not come back scared me. I remember being upset.

Many days passed, and I did not get any visits from my *nookum*. Although she had told me before she was not going to visit for a while, I hopefully watched for her. When she did come back she said she was going to tell me another story that happened before I was placed at the residential school.

Her story was:

> *"You went through a sacred ceremony performed by a medicine man and that ceremony is always going to be with you. No matter what the priest or nuns put you through, the* Medewewin *will stay with you."*

I was very proud, and went around repeating the story to my friends. It was a mistake. One of the sisters heard about it and asked me what *"medewewin"* meant. I nervously tried to answer, but my stumbling words made it worse.

She grabbed me by the back of my dress, and pulled me to the principal's office. The Sister told the principal I had participated in a pagan ritual. They took me to the punishing room.

The straps were kept there. There was a leather strap, a paddle, a horse harness, a cat-o'-nine-tails with a round handle, and a one-inch wide piece of lumber used for the beatings. Sometimes they just hit your fingers so your nails would change colour and fall off. Other times they beat you, alternating between the leather strap and the stick. I don't know how long the beating took.

The next thing I remember is waking up on my bed. One of the older girls had been assigned to watch over me. There was so much pain. Finally, when I was able to get up, I was allowed to go down and join the girls in the playroom. The supervisor came with one of the older girls to tell me I must never talk about having done the *Medewewin* ceremony again—or I would go to Hell. Being shamed in front of the other girls hurt me as deeply as the beating. I had wanted to be an angel, but I had become an evil pagan.

My family must have heard about the beating. I remember my *nindede* coming and carrying me out of sight so the Sister couldn't see us. *Nindede* turned away while *nookum* examined my body for bruises. After her report, *nindede* left me alone with *nookum*. He walked to the school, and went in to confront the principal. It didn't do any good. *Nindede* was threatened with jail if he took me away from the school. It must have been very painful for them to leave me there. I begged my *nindede* to take me with him but it couldn't be. The principal had the power so I stayed, waiting for release.

SUMMER VACATION

After my baptism, my *nindede* promised he would be back for me. The wonderful day finally came with joy. He came to bring me home for summer holidays.

I remember sitting with my *nookum* by the open fire as she prepared supper for the family. I would help a bit, but mostly I got to hear her tell stories from the past.

Nookum had grown up on Powwow Island. She talked about her childhood—playing with other girls, swimming in the clear waters, making dolls out of leather. To this day, when I visit the island, I envision her as a girl, living free as a traditional *Anishinaabe*. Summer vacation was my time also. It was the vision of coming back to the bush and my people that kept me alive during the school year.

My *nindede* remarried. Mostly I stayed with my *nookum* during holidays. She did spoil me, but I also learned from her. I didn't learn as much as I could have, because I was afraid of being punished again for being a pagan. It was the Elder's job to teach the young ones. It must have been hard. We didn't respect them, as we should have. We were told at residential school we would go to Hell if we listened to them and their teachings.

Summertime allowed me to lose myself in the bush. To this day, I come alive when trees surround me. There is a connection to the land that non-aboriginal people cannot understand. We are tied to Mother Earth, who nourishes us with Her gifts. They flow to us in the same way a mother flows nourishment to her baby through the umbilical cord. We are safe within Her womb. This is why pollution is dangerous. It poisons our womb. We will suffer because of it. Preserving our world is more important than money, or ownership, or our personal wants. It is greed and carelessness that poisons our Mother Earth.

The bush held berries. I still love the taste of wild fruit. We would pick berries—sometimes alone, sometimes with others. The picking was hard, but it was good work with lots of laughter as we filled our buckets. Some berries were eaten on the spot. The rest would be dried or preserved for future treats. Nothing is as good as berries on bannock! If our families brought us bannock during the school year, the staff took it away from us. We were told our traditional foods would make us sick. In the summertime we feasted; we didn't get sick.

The blueberries also were sold. A cup would earn me five cents. There would be big berry-picking expeditions. As a child I used to wonder how everyone knew where to go. Dozens and dozens of canoes would suddenly head out onto the lake out at the same time. Later I found out the scouts located the spots and sent back word. There were many places we would go to—and all of us would go. Everyone shared the gifts of Mother Earth. No one hid away their bounty.

I liked to wander away alone in the bush, and I did get lost a couple of times. When I was about eight years old, I started following a road and ended up at Dogtooth Lake. I stood on the shore looking for my people when some other *Anishinaabe* spotted me. They were taking a taxi into town and stopped to rescue me. I wasn't worried. I was young, and happily had blueberries to eat. But, they knew I shouldn't be alone, so they took me back to my own people.

There were hundreds of us on these berry-picking trips—or maybe it just seemed like hundreds to a child like me. Our fleet of canoes would take us to Rushing River. There, we would disembark. The men would then slide the canoes down the rapids. I wanted to go in the canoe with my *mishomis* (grandfather) but it was too dangerous. The women and children would portage down the river to our gathering spot at Sand Point. It was a beautiful camp with sandy beaches and warm waters. As a reward, for helping with the picking, we would each be given a dollar. In those days a penny bought a whole bag of candy, so a dollar made us rich.

Once at the camp spot, I found five dollars in my *nookum*'s tent. My friends and I took a canoe and paddled to the store. Five dollars bought us more candy than we had ever seen before. Once back at camp, I divided the candy into shares. Each friend was given a little bundle, but they started to count the candy and argued over who got the most. Finally, they grabbed the remaining candy that was still in the paper bag. I screamed at them to give me my candy back and my *nookum* came. She figured out where the money had come from and said we would have to take it back to the store to get the money returned. I cried that I wanted all my candy and the girls started throwing it at me. It rained candy down on me. The candy wasn't good any more, and my friends left me. I learned a lesson from that: Greed makes trouble between friends.

Summer was also for fishing, accompanied by swimming. The lake called us. The adults would net the fish while the children played. The fish was eaten immediately, or smoked for our food stores. The children's job during the smoking process was to chase the dogs away from the fish being smoked on the racks over the fires. If we didn't watch, the dogs would snatch away our food. There were many, many dogs, so we were kept busy with this task.

When the work was done, we would chase around camp, playing tag, ball, and jacks. When dusk came the drums began. It was different then. People danced for joy, not for honorariums. As the night grew darker, the storytellers would begin. Many times we would nod off to the sounds of their stories. The stories were for teaching, and sometimes for fun. The stories were also told during the waiting times—while we waited for rice or berries to ripen, or when the weather kept us from our work.

Back at our cabin, I would help my *nookum* with gathering medicines. Like her husband, she was a respected healer. A message would be sent to her about someone's illness. Sometimes runners brought the news. That was how we communicated. A runner would take messages between camps. When *nookum's* help was needed, she would put on her apron with the big pocket. She had made one for me too. I would slip a book into my pocket because that seemed more interesting than what she had to show me. She had so much knowledge, but I was too disrespectful to pay attention. Some things I learned, more by her persistence than my interest. Plants are medicines that can heal us if we know which ones to use and how to prepare them. So many of the places we went are now gone—replaced by roads, buildings, and parking lots. Without the plants we cannot heal ourselves.

After blueberry season, the summer began turning into fall. It was time to return to school. My older brother and sister did not have to return to their residential school. I was happy for them. I was not happy for me, so my *nindede* thought up a way to make me happy.

My *nindede* took me to town as a treat before my return to school. We could see a movie at the Bijou and eat in a café. Some places we weren't allowed to eat in because we were Indian. But, we were allowed to spend our money in shops on things like combs, skin cream, and barrettes. Like most girls, I was very excited about these things. The nuns always told students who were allowed to go to town with their parents that they must not buy anything fancy. It was a sin.

I remember looking at a pretty blue dress in a store. It had a tiny collar and shiny decorations down the front. It was beautiful to me. My big eyes must have told *nindede* how much I wanted the dress. *Nindede* asked the sales lady if I could try it on. I did—and it fit perfectly—so he bought it for me. He also bought me new shiny black patent shoes with a buckle on the side. I was so proud of these beautiful things and I wanted to share my excitement with my friends at school; *Nindede* gave me a reason to go back to the hated school.

BACK TO SCHOOL

I went back to school clutching my *nindede's* gifts. My friends ran over to meet me, asking what I was carrying. I showed them everything, including my special blue dress. The Sister saw. She took the dress from my hands, looked at it, and walked away. I was too afraid of her to ask. I never saw the dress again. I also never told my father what happened to that special dress. We were not allowed to bring fancy things to school.

Stripped of my beautiful clothes, I was taken to the bathroom. I tried to tell the Sister that *nookum* had already given me a bath before I my family brought me back to school, but no one listened. My hair was scrubbed with kerosene or coal oil. It burned. I screamed, and tried to escape, but it was hopeless.

Every girl received the same treatment. It was supposed to cleanse us of lice. If a girl was found to have lice, all of her hair was shaved off.

Then, I was pushed into the too hot bathtub. After the Sister was done with me, the girl assisting with the bathing helped me out of the tub. I got dressed in the school uniform. I remember telling the big girl I wanted my new clothes back. My new clothing, and my pride, were forcibly taken in this battle.

The next day I was taken to the nurse's office. The nurse started her examination from my head touching and feeling slowly down towards my stomach. She didn't stop there. Her fingers went down to where we were told not to touch ourselves. She was hurting me. Yet, when she asked if it felt good, I had no choice but to say "yes" for fear I would be hit. *Nokomis* taught my sisters and I we must not undress before anybody, especially boys and men. Even at school we were not supposed to expose ourselves to other girls. Why was the nurse allowed to poke her fingers there? That was my first time being "examined". Later, I experienced the Sister also touching me there in our special parts. She also asked if it felt good and I would have to answer "yes". To this day I don't know if these examinations were sexual assaults. I don't know why the Sister had to touch us there. Why did we have to tell the priest we were touching ourselves there and ask for forgiveness when we never did it? It was done to all of us, so we kept silent in our confusion and shame.

There was a new girl in our class. She was put into the seat next to me. She couldn't stop crying. She sobbed in Ojibwe that she wanted her mother to come and take her home. Speaking our language was punishable. I didn't answer her for fear of being hit. An older girl came over and whispered to her in our language. She was brave to do so. Eventually the new student realized she would not be rescued. She would often say she was going to run away. She was our friend, so we said we would go with her. We all promised not to tell anyone. Around this promise, the five of us became best friends.

The nurse came into the dining room and announced some of us would be called to see the dentist. I didn't know what would happen because I didn't know what a dentist was. Number Seven was called. That was me. The principal and sisters didn't use our names, just numbers. I was known as Number Seven.

Right after dinner we were ordered to line up and wait our turn. I heard screaming. A girl came out of the nurse's room holding her face. Some of the children had to be forced into the room. I got scared and tried to run back toward the playroom, but a nun caught me and carried me in. I was forced into a chair. My mouth was pried open and someone sprayed something into it. The dentist then pulled out one of my left teeth.

I was taken back to the dormitory. The pain was awful. My face swelled with infection. Five of us were taken to the hospital, suffering from the effects of the dental work. To this day I am fearful of dentists.

One time we were preparing for our evening prayers when all of a sudden the lights flickered and the room got completely dark. I stopped what I was doing, as did the other girls, and stayed in silence—frozen.

When I stood up to investigate, strange noises like moans and other eerie sounds, were coming from the hallway. Something came toward us, and the lights came on. In front of us was a devil. It was dressed in black, horns on its head, a tail behind it, and carrying a pitchfork. We were terrified.

Girls screamed and cried out as they tried to get away from the creature. We formed a writhing ball because we could not escape. A voice ordered us to be silent. We knew how to obey and held our breath in unison. The devil announced it had a list of names of whom it would take to Hell. We began crying hysterically in fear. The sound of a strap hitting wood gained order. The devil disappeared. Several girls had been injured in the frenzy and were sent to the dormitory to recuperate. Even Halloween was an excuse to terrorize us.

One time when we were playing outside one of the missionaries came toward us with a snake. We ran away from him, but he followed us, continuing to chase us with the fearful creature. He did finally catch one girl. She screamed as he draped the snake over her. To this day I am also terrified of snakes. My brother has tried to assure me they are harmless creatures, but he hasn't yet convinced me.

Christmas was coming. At Bible Study we were each given an assignment. We were to make dolls. I made my doll with white material and golden hair. I had already learned that being White was good, and I wanted my doll to be special. Brown skin and black hair would brand my doll as Indian, as it did me. Being Indian meant being a dirty squaw. The nuns had worked hard to teach us to be ladies. They had to remind us continually, or we would slide right into their alleged ugly behaviours.

Once the beautiful blonde doll was finished the nuns took it away. We knew not to question it because that would only mean a beating. At the Christmas concert we each received a candy cane and an orange. Santa gave me a package. Inside was my precious doll. I was proud of my doll and carried her everywhere until summertime. Eventually its white skin got too dirty and it was thrown out, but it was my first Christmas gift and it was a happy memory. My great-grandchildren can't imagine why I would be so excited to get my own gift back. So much was taken from us; we never expected to get anything back. I am glad my children, grandchildren and great-grandchildren do not know how this feels.

ESCAPE

One day in October my class was allowed in the playground. There were strict rules about the playground. We had to stay in sight of the supervising sister. There were red stakes marking the edge of the grounds. There was a hillside beyond the stakes and the Sister warned us, if we stepped past the markers, we would roll down the hill and into the lake.

On this particular day, my friends and I sat down near the red stakes to talk in the fresh air. One of us decided to check the hill's slope to see if it was really as dangerous as the Sister said. We followed our friend to watch. We could see no danger. Three of the girls backed up to the safety of the red-staked boundary. Our new friend, who had told us that she was going to run away, stayed on the hillside. I was between them. The girls behind me called down to us to hurry up before we got caught. Then they warned us it was time to line up and go back to school.

I scrambled up the hill, but when I got there everyone was gone. I knew we were in big trouble, and stood frozen in fear. My new friend reached me and saw the empty yard. She quickly turned and ran down toward the road. Too scared to return to the school, I ran after her. We ran and ran until we reached the bush. We walked onward, parallel to the road but hidden by the trees.

We headed toward Indian House. I was so very happy we were out of school. Freedom filled me. I knew we could not go to our families' tents because they would have to take us back to school. They had no choice.

We stayed hidden as we walked. When we heard the school bell ringing in the distance we knew it was time for evening prayers. Night was coming. It got colder. We didn't have sweaters or coats since it had been a warm afternoon. We were hungry.

We headed toward town. I knew we could find food behind the restaurants and grocery stores. We sneaked down the alleys and took what we could carry to our hiding place. There, we ate and slept. For the next several days, we kept moving. We would wait until dark, sneak into town for supplies, and then bed down in a new spot. We must have been good at hiding because my *nookum* later told me the Mounties and our own people searched for us for days.

Then the rain started. It came down steady. We knew we needed shelter. Our families were at Indian House in their tents, so I realized our family cabin would be empty. We arrived wet, cold, and miserable. We dropped into a deep sleep and didn't stir until morning. We made a meager breakfast from what had been left behind. We left with borrowed jackets. We searched for other unlocked cabins. After more of our wandering, I was seized with loneliness. I wanted my *nookum* and my *nindede*. I could not be with them as long as we kept running. I wanted to go to them. I knew they must be worried.

My friend refused to go with me. She warned me the police would get me if I showed myself. I didn't know what the police were so she explained. She said it was police who had come to take her away from her parents. They brought her to the awful school. If she saw the police coming, she said she would jump in the lake. I knew I could not jump in the lake with her. I didn't know how to swim very well. So, we stayed where we were for the night.

The next morning we planned to head toward Indian House again. We would stay hidden and figure out what to do closer to our families. We were about to leave when my friend suddenly stopped. She pointed at two men in the distance, and we hid. We watched them go into *nookum's* cabin. We crept closer to see who they were. I realized one was my uncle. I wanted to call out to him, but my friend put her hand over my mouth to silence me.

The men looked around, and then finally left the area. There was nothing left to eat so we returned to walking through the woods. We didn't get far before three men and a dog came into our view. We tried to hide, but the dog ran barking at us. We jumped up and ran, but we were soon caught and returned to the school.

Years later my *nookum* told me about this time. She and my *nindede* were worried when they were told I was missing. Having already lost my two sisters, they feared the worst for me also. It must have been very, very hard on them.

At the school, the principal, four nuns, and the police met us. We were taken directly into the principal's office and waited while they talked. When the police finally left, we knew what was coming.

The principal led us to the punishing room. Two nuns held me to make sure I couldn't run away. The other two nuns held my friend. My friend was taken in first. It was silent, but then I heard the strap hitting her. She screamed with pain and cried out, "No, no, don't." I struggled to escape but the nuns held me firmly. Then the screaming stopped and there was just whimpering. I stood shaking, knowing I would be next.

The door opened and my friend was led out naked—under a white sheet—and shaved bald. The look on her face still haunts me. I broke loose but the nuns caught me. Kicking and screaming, I was dragged into the punishing room.

One of the nuns held me down. I felt the strap hitting my legs. Then hands undressed me. Naked, I squirmed away, crawling on my hands and knees. The strap whistled down again and again. I was pulled up on a stool where the nuns held me while the principal shaved my hair. I was pulled to my feet—naked and bald—and a sheet was draped over me too.

I was taken with my friend to the playroom. The girls were lined up, and stood silently. We were ordered to walk and stop in front of each girl so they could see and learn from our punishment. We made our way around the room.

The dinner bell rang and we were led to the dining room for the boys to see our shame. Everyone had to look at what happens to anyone who dares to run away. I was nine years old.

I was in terrible pain from the beating but I was not allowed to lie down. They sent us out to the playground. I sought refuge in the outside toilet. I lay there, very still, for a long time. The Sister tried to make me leave the outhouse, and then the girls tried to coax me out. I was in shock and couldn't bring myself to move. Finally, I did get up. My friend and I were not allowed contact with each other again after that.

My *nindede* arrived at the school with my *nookum* and older sister. The women took me aside to examine me as a nun stood nearby to watch. My *nindede* came back into the room and sadly told me I had to stay. He promised they would increase their visits, and I would not be punished like that again, but those assurances weren't enough. I pleaded and begged. I cried helplessly while I was led back into the school.

As I entered the school, I vomited all over the floor in fear but I was not punished. I refused to eat but I was not punished. Nighttime was the worst. I was afraid to go to sleep. When I finally dropped off, I would jerk awake screaming. I woke up all the girls night after night. I started wetting the bed again, and still I wasn't punished.

The Sister ordered a bed to be put next to mine, and one of the bigger girls was told to stay with me to keep me quiet. It didn't help. Nothing helped. One morning I was told to stay in bed until the doctor came.

Eventually I settled down. I had lost hope. I was forced to accept I would be staying at the school. I joined the girls in the playroom and returned to class and chores.

Even though the Sister had instructed my friend and I to stay apart, we managed to sneak little meetings and talks together. Our hair grew back. We returned to the dreary routine.

MORE SCHOOL

The bells told us what to do. There were morning bells, meal bells, and prayer bells. Everything was regimented. It was so different from our lives during summer holidays.

Now I walk over the land where residential school stood and it seems so small. Once it was a three-storey building that held our lives within its walls. Now there is nothing left of it. But when I shut my eyes, the building stands firmly etched into my memory.

You entered through a veranda that ran along the front of the school. On the first floor there was a classroom, a kitchen, a laundry room, the priest's dining room, the Sisters' dining room, the students' dining room, and the principal's office. The boys' playroom was also on the first floor. On the second floor were the sewing room, another classroom, the girls' playroom, the nuns' quarters, and a chapel. The dormitories were on the top floor. Outside there was a woodshed, a stable, and carriage shed. These areas were the boys' responsibility. Chores, as well as the school and playground times, were scheduled to keep the boys and girls apart as much as possible.

We were not allowed to even look at the boys when we came in contact with each other. Even our breasts were bound up so our femininity would not show. When I was about twelve years old, there was a boy from Sabaskong who would smile at me. I guess he liked me. The inevitable happened—the nuns noticed our shy glances.

I wasn't the only one scooped up by the nuns in retribution for looking at a boy. I was taken, with a few other girls, and we were forced to put on boy's overalls and caps. This was very strange, but we did what we were ordered to do. Dressed like boys, we were paraded around to shame us in front of the girls and boys. Then we were taken aside and warned boys only wanted to touch us in bad ways. If we allowed them to do that we would be Jezebels or hussies.

None of us knew what a Jezebel or hussy was. It was confusing. The nuns would call us Jezebels when they were angry with us. The word sounded funny to us, so we began teasing each other with it. Soon enough Mother Superior found out and ordered us to stop using the word. Of course, the more defiant ones kept it up and were punished. There never was an explanation of what the word meant and why we were being punished. Years later I looked up the words in a dictionary to try to make sense out of what they were accusing us of. The dictionary said a Jezebel was a whore or prostitute. None of us were that.

There was a girl who from time to time would fall into an epileptic seizure. The nuns would have us beat her with sticks and kick her, because they thought she was possessed by the Devil. They believed if we hurt her body then the Devil would leave it. To this day I am ashamed of having taken part in this. We did what we were told, but it was wrong.

By the time I was fourteen, I understood much more. I heard the whispers of the girls saying "*aambegish niibo waan* (I want to die)". I didn't want to die, so I became rebellious—fighting back when they called me a dirty Indian, a squaw, and a pagan who was destined to burn in Hell. I refused to cry no matter how I hurt from the beatings. I ran away again and again.

When *nookum* came to visit me one day, I told her I was not going to stay at the school anymore. She warned it was winter and I would freeze if I ran away. I didn't care anymore. She knew I was serious and spoke with my father. The principal met with my *nindede* and then I was called into the office. I was given the choice of going to live with my *nindede* and my stepmother in Onigaming, or being sent to reform school, which was a jail for disobedient young people. The choice was easy. I chose freedom.

RELEASE

I left the school with my *nindede*. I was finally free to live with my people—but my freedom did have a cost. Being released did not mean I could do as I pleased. When I refused to do something, an explanation was given as to why it had to be done. The Elders told us we had much to learn. Listening, learning and doing are how we share knowledge and pass it on to the younger members of our community. It was different from residential school—we weren't expected to obey blindly. We were expected to contribute to the community—and our contributions were valued.

When we are young, our energy should be channeled into worthwhile activities. When we are fully grown, our skills support each member of the community. When we age, and cannot do so many chores, we share our knowledge and wisdom as Elders. This wisdom channels the energy of our youth into activities that turn the circle of our traditional life.

My life was best when *nindede* was around, but sometimes he worked away from home. *Nindede* worked at Canadian Pacific Railway camp for twenty-five years. He also did various jobs including repair work and guiding.

Nindede cut pulp with his brothers. Our family members were known to be good workers, so they were always hired first. Even my *nookum* worked cleaning houses in town. When I was very young, she used to take me with her. The ladies of the house would give me treats while she cleaned for them. I also learned how to cut pulpwood by helping my grandparents. I was taught how to use an axe and swede saw at an early age. Most of the women helped their partners in the bush. I didn't really like domestic work, so I wanted to go and help my grandparents instead. My *mishomis* said I could cut pulpwood as long as a tree didn't fall on me and hurt me. We were taught how to work safely, but once chainsaws came into use the women were told they could not help anymore. That didn't stop me—I just learned how to use a power saw properly. My thought was if I could learn it, I could do it!

At Sabaskong my family had a big log house with two rooms. We had everything we needed and were never hungry. We worked hard to provide for ourselves. There was a big garden that kept us supplied with potatoes, corn, and other vegetables. I remember the great stores of potatoes after harvest. We would dry the corn for winter. Some of the dried corn would be ground through a meat grinder. To get a really fine corn flour, we would put the ground corn into a sack and pound it into a powder. The only supplies we bought were things like wheat flour, sugar, tea, and baking powder. We didn't need much. Trips to town were rare.

Mother Earth provided us with berries (wild strawberries, raspberries and gooseberries, in addition to the blueberries), fish (walleye, sturgeon, and bass) and meat (deer, elk, moose, geese, ducks, rabbits, and bears). Up in the trees surrounding our house, we stashed the meat to protect it from hungry animals. Nothing went to waste. Even the animal skin and bones had a purpose in our world. Skins became shelter, clothing and footwear, as well as drums. Bones were carved into tools used to scrape the fur off of the animal hides. Furs kept us warm and gave us an income for those few store bought items we enjoyed. I always liked candy when I was young. I could never get enough. I am diabetic now and paying the price for not sticking with our traditional diet.

My stepmother knew how to use wild plants to flavour the food well—mint, strawberry leaves, chokecherry bark. Everything on Earth was put here for us by the Creator. Stepmother had never gone to school. She had learned the old ways well from her Elders. I didn't like to be around her, though, so I didn't learn her ways. I'm still trying to recover some of the knowledge she had. I blame myself for wasting this knowledge in my youth, but all youth lack wisdom in this regard.

Every spring and fall there was a big feast at Sabaskong. Hundreds of *Anishinaabe* would gather to share and celebrate for four days. They would come by canoe since there was no road. My job was to make bannock. *Nindede* would make a big fire pit and put flat rocks around it. I would bake the bannock on the rocks to keep the feast supplied in the quantities required. I was also responsible for cooking the white rice and raisins. Other girls cooked other things. We all had our specialties. I was still young enough to resent having to cook, and watch the younger children, while the adults were feasting. I wanted to be there with them. On the fourth day, the girls who had been preparing the food were brought to the feast. That's when we would be honoured for our work.

After the spring feast, we would begin gathering at Indian House where Anicinabe Park is now. We would put up tents and live together for the summer. It was a great gathering. We looked forward to it every year. Family and friends met up again to share the work and enjoy each other's company.

Over the summer, the adults would be netting fish and preserving some for their winter stores. Then there would be berry picking, followed by wild rice gathering. The nights were full of laughter. There wasn't drinking at Indian House. If someone showed up intoxicated, we were surprised. The police would be called and they would be put into jail for seven days. Drunkenness was not approved of. The chief would patrol the grounds himself to make sure everyone was being good to each other. It was his responsibility to watch over us.

Card playing was popular. Occasionally a small bit of money was bet on the game. It would be fun until a police car appeared.

As soon as a cruiser was spotted, the cards would disappear. I didn't understand this so I asked my *nookum*. She told me gambling was not allowed in any reservation. There were lots of rules like that.

My *nindede* and his in-laws would sneak me money as an allowance, and I guarded it with my life. I could slip away from my responsibilities for town treats. They knew how my stepmother acted toward me, so they tried to give me extra things. I liked store bought things like rubber boots and shoes. My stepmother would make me beautiful moccasins but I wouldn't wear them. I was foolish like most young people.

Even though I liked store-bought treats, I didn't like to go to the store. Discrimination was bad in those days. There were only certain places we were allowed to go into. The older White kids would wait around to hurt us. They would yell at us, throw rocks at us, and sometimes beat us up. I would carry my little brother while we passed them, to try to keep him safe in my arms.

When I was around sixteen or seventeen, I had the honour of meeting the Elder who have given me my name. *Nokomis* had already told me who he was. It is our way to wait until an Elder is ready to speak. Sometimes it is a short time, and sometimes it is a long wait, but it is always a wait undertaken with respect for the Elder's time.

I happened to pass by his tent when he invited me to sit down by the fire with him and his wife. They served me tea and bannock. He started to tell me the same story *nookum* told me about my naming.

When it was time for me to leave he asked me if I would sit for a while longer. He wanted to say a few words. He went on to tell me about a prophecy that was going to happen in the future. I did not believe him and soon forgot about it. As I got older, the words came back to me:

Girl I have given you a name, which will have a strong impact in your future. You might forget it but as you get older it will return to remind you someday.

In the future, you will see many dawns in your life. Before that happens you will experience many abuses, but you will survive them. You will go stumbling into many obstacles, but you will manage to get up. You will go through much suffering due to your own doing. Finally, you will realize you had enough and will ask for help. Someone you will not see will hear and help you. Then you will see your hair turn white—and you will see your children grow, also your grandchildren and great-grandchildren. When that time comes, you will remember what you have been told.

I went back many times to the words the Elder gave me. He also told me of other things. Some things I still keep inside me because they are so frightening. Many of his prophecies have come true.

Toward the end of summer, our scouts would locate the rice paddies ready for picking. The *jeemonnug* (canoes) would be launched and the adults would leave for harvesting. While the adults were away, I was given the responsibility of my four younger brothers, as well as the cooking and cleaning. At fourteen, I resented being left at camp to do this, but I did love my brothers, and they loved me. When I got older I was able to go rice picking with the adults. Most of all, my people loved *maanomin* (wild rice). It was a special gift to the *Anishinaabe* from the Creator.

At the harvest sites, one person would pole the canoe through the wild rice beds. The partner would pull the stalks into the boat and then knock the grain kernels into the canoe with ricing sticks. Both the guiding and the picking were hard work and your arms could get very tired. When the boats were finally filled they would return to our camp.

At camp, the rice would be spread out to dry. We would pick out the sticks and leaves mixed in during harvesting. Then rice would be roasted over the fire. This gave it the smoky rich flavour so special to our people. You had to stir it constantly so it would not scorch during the roasting process. Again—strong arms were necessary.

Once the roasting was completed, a pit would be dug. Hides would be laid to keep the rice clean. Then drums would begin. For this purpose, hand drums usually guided the dancers. I was nervous about the drums for a long time, because of what I was taught at school by the nuns. I would have to force myself to stay calm once the drums began. All of the fearful words would swirl around within my head—pagan, evil, demonic. It was many years before the drums brought me comfort.

At the fur-lined rice pit, dancers in moccasins would jump in and tread lightly over the rice. It was very difficult to do it just right and it took a long time, so dancers took turns. The purpose of the dancing was to separate the hulls from the chaff.

After the dancing, we would put the rice in baskets. The wind would help us sort the rice. We would toss the basket contents into the air and the breeze would blow the chaff away. The broken rice fell onto the ground and the good rice fell back into the basket. The rice was then ready to be stored for the winter. *Manoominikewin* (making rice) was a lot of work, but it was made easier because we all worked together. Each family would be given about a dozen hundred-pound bags for their winter supplies.

Every season had a purpose. Fall was about preparing for the winter. There was no refrigeration so everything was preserved by natural methods. We canned the wild fruit. Blueberries were sundried and used like raisins. The corn was dried and pounded by hand into flour. While the women worked together at Indian House, the men would hunt.

As winter approached, the big game had to be hunted. With the men gone, there was still no time for idleness. We made moccasins and warm winter wear. I was responsible for knitting the mitts, toques and scarves for the boys. This gave my stepmother more time to make the beaded and fringed leather jackets that the tourists bought. Her skill brought money to the family.

When the freshly killed moose and deer were brought home from the hunt, we flew into action. My stepmother and her sister would unload the carcass to begin the butchering of the meat. Some was cut into thin slices and hung over open fires until they became leathery condensed nutrition. Hunters and trappers, who had to travel light, used this smoked meat. The bones from the animals were sharpened and used to scrape the fur off of the animal hides. Once we separated the fur from the hide, the tanning process took about three weeks. Every bit of the animal was used out of respect for the life sacrificed to us for our people's survival.

As winter set in, our outside work became more limited. We would set snares in the snow, and nets under the ice for fresh meat and fish. My *nindede*'s in-laws had a trap line, and sometimes I was able to go with him. I loved my time alone with Dad. We would hitch up the horse and sleigh to travel from home to Big Grassy and then westward. Our sleigh runners would throw up snow in an arc behind us, leaving a trail of our passage across the snowy land and the frozen ice.

I rode my first snow machine recently. I wonder what my father would think of that. It went fast but it was noisy. Too noisy—you can't talk to each other, and you are scaring all of the animals away from you.

It took about a day to reach the traps. I thought it was a great time but *nindede*, being wiser, knew the dangers and worried constantly about my safety. So much could go wrong but when you are young, you don't know so much.

In our tradition the parents must teach their children how to survive. There were instructions on what do if you broke through the ice. I learned to always carry matches and a small pebble with me when I travelled through the bush. Sucking on the pebble gives energy. Matches to quickly light a fire can save your life. There were lessons on how to skin muskrat and beaver without cutting through the carcass. I learned to make a *bajiishka'ogaan* (tipi) frame over a fire to smoke the hide, as well as the meat. It was important learning, and being alone with my *nindede* made the lessons special. He taught me with love and his lessons still live in my heart.

My first hunting trip with my father was an experience. I had been so excited to go with him, but the reality of killing left me shaken. *Nindede* knew how I was feeling and he taught me we kill only to survive. When animals are killed, we give thanks for their lives. We have to respect their sacrifice for our benefit. This means we never waste the gift of their lives. This respect for all creation is the most important law of the *Anishabe*.

It was getting late, so *nindede* decided we needed to spend the night. Fortunately there was a cabin nearby we could stay in for comfort. To protect the animal carcass from predators, we had to set a fire to burn throughout the night. My father used the evening to teach me one more lesson for survival. I learned to make a leanto for those times when I was not be able to find my way home at night.

Nindede looked for a tree blown down by the wind. If a person can crawl under the tree, it is the right choice. An offering of tobacco is made to the trees that give up their branches for our shelter. Dried sticks are gathered to secure around the tree shelter. Boughs of balsam and spruce are placed over the sticks to roof the shelter. More soft boughs are placed inside for sleeping comfort. I was taught to use branches from several trees, so one tree alone is not be stripped. This is the respect we must give to all living things. Traditional wisdom taught us not to strip our resources because Mother Earth cannot replenish them. Clear-cutting and strip mining go against this wisdom. Money can't replace our woodlands.

I also used ice fishing as an excuse to be with my *nindede*. We would make two holes and thread through them using a branch with an *ahsubb* (net). There were always fish in the *ahsubb* when we pulled the branch out. Fish could be smoked or canned for our food supply. My stepmother made really good canned sucker. I wished I had learned that from her because it was tastier than any salmon you buy today. Sucker-head soup was often served and tasted much better than it sounds. My brothers loved bannock with raisins. I always had to make it for them in our heavy cast iron frying pans on our wood cook stove. I grumbled—but secretly I was proud of my bannock-making skill.

FROZEN TEARS

One time my n*ookum* took me rice picking because she wanted me to spend time with my sister. It was an adventure. The *jeemon-nug* headed toward Whiteshell, It took many days because we stopped to harvest ripened rice and late berries as we moved along. We travelled together in a big fleet of boats. A few of our people had motorboats and they helped pull slower canoes along. No one was left behind and everyone worked together. *Anishinaabe* people always moved together as a tribe. They shared and helped each other. It was what was expected of us as community members.

On this trip my *nookum* decided it was time to speak to me about my attitude. We were north of Clearwater Bay and I was helping her to prepare supper at the campfire. She spoke about how I had grown up rebelling against school. The anger and hatred I had in my heart was giving me a bad attitude. As long as it stayed in my heart, I would face many obstacles because I wouldn't listen, and I didn't believe, and I didn't have respect. This would be trouble for me all of my life if I did not change.

I ignored her words but she went on: "You have ears but you do not hear. You have eyes but you do not see. You have a heart that is a stone."

Stubbornly, I turned away from her. She was always trying to get emotions out of me. Mine were frozen. Two of my older sisters had died and I showed nothing. School taught me to show nothing. Becoming hard was how I survived.

Being hard did not protect me from the loss of my *nindede*. A runner came to Indian House to tell us my father was at the hospital. The woman who was managing Crow Lake Lodge had hit him with her car as he was walking down the highway at night. I don't know why he was on that road. He might have been trying to come see us for a visit.

I stayed in my uncle's tent. I felt heavy like a stone. I started to bleed even though it wasn't my moon time. I must have been in shock with the loss of my *nindede*. My aunt took me to the Mass for him at the chapel. I stayed, staring at his body, but felt nothing. It was like I wasn't a part of it. Even *nookum* could not reach through the stone that encased me.

After my father's death it was time to go to the pulpwood camp. That's when I realized my *nindede* would not be coming with us. What had happened had been real. The stone around my heart cracked under the power of my pain. As always, *nookum* was there beside me.

Nookum spoke about how my father would not want me to be sad. She said it was time I accepted he would not be coming back. I tried to walk away from her but she pulled me back down to sit beside her.

She began to sing a healing song, and something changed inside me. When she was done her song, she put her hand out and touched my face. My *nookum* said, "Your face is wet." I did not know what was happening.

Nokomis smiled and said, "You are crying. Finally your feelings are back. Now you will be able to get rid of your anger. Carrying it was a burden. Now you can know love."

Then *nookum* gave me a teaching:

> *"Crying is good. Tears have been given by the Creator to use when we are hurting or suffering. Tears are for healing. Tears help us to gain strength to erase what has happened to you. Tears give us courage to stand up*

against violence and abuse. You will see many tears in your lifetime. Always let them out. There are also tears of joy for when you see your first child or the approach of someone you love. Let the happiness of tears out also. It is right to shed tears."

WOMANHOOD

I went to the work camp with my uncle and my partner. I loved bush work. My job was to de-limb the felled trees and cut them into four-foot pieces the men would pile. I used a swede saw. I was little, but I worked as hard as the men, and I earned my own money. It suited me to be independent.

I also was finally allowed to use a gun, but I never did take a liking to it. It was useful but I would rather snare than shoot. Unfortunately, I liked wild meat, and the surest way to bring home moose meat is to use a gun.

I took to drinking when I was twenty-two years old. I had a man who drank and I got fed up with being the only sober person. I'm not blaming him for how I came to be. I downed everything fast because then I didn't feel the pain. Pain came with sobriety. My man was abusive—drunk or sober. People would talk about it. My *nookum* complained, "Every time I see Nancy she has a shiner."

I figured I was tough enough to take it. I had been a human punching bag since I was three years old. I expected it—and was even proud I didn't back down, no matter what was done to me. Now I know this kind of toughness was part of the wall that kept me from a good life.

Sometimes when my partner was beating me, *nookum* would throw herself over me and take the beating herself. She loved me that much. She told me to leave him but I didn't have options. I couldn't keep my seasonal bush work without him. Women didn't get hired alone for bush work. I was afraid to look for a job in town because of the racism. I didn't think I had any skills of my own. I worried about what to do with my kids. Finally, my *nookum* said, "Go before he kills you." I listened.

My brother worked in a tourist camp so I went to work there for a while cleaning cabins. As was tradition, my children went to live with their grandparents. I worked around the area—Dryden, Kenora, Lake of the Woods. I could find work but I also could find alcohol.

I was a binger—working for a while and then going on a drunk that kept me on the streets for days on end. Even though it was generally dangerous for a woman to be on the streets, my tough-ness kept me safer than most. I was tiny but even the cops would back away from me. I had attitude driven by my rebelliousness and anger.

There was much in my life that hurt me deeply. I can live with it now, but there were times when I would look back and anger would fill me.

My *nookum* gave me a teaching that eventually brought me out of the pain of my past and into a better life. It took me a while to live like *nookum* advised, but after time and making the right choices, I did live. Her guiding words were as follows:

> *"Do not look back on the life of abuse you experienced when you were young. Hate, anger, despair and depres-sion will settle down on you and the weight of these memories will have a very negative effect on your future. You can have a good future if you let all go."*

Alcohol played two roles in my life; drinking helped me to forget but it also became part of my revenge against all those who had hurt me. I blamed the Creator, the Roman Catholic school, and everyone but myself. I didn't take any responsibility for the addiction. Eventually I realized it was me who took the bottle and me who drank it down.

Being a woman in those days was hard. You always had to fight to be respected, and even then you were kept away from many things. It wasn't like that for our women before residential schools. Our tradition respects both men and women. It was Christianity that taught us about being Jezebels and about being ashamed of our bodies. Women brought sin into the world according to the priests. In our *Anishinaabe* tradition, women bring life into the world and are respected, as is Mother Earth.

We are slowly recovering respect according to the old ways. Women are beginning to drum and sing. It is awesome. My own niece became our first female chief of the Grand Council. My daughters and granddaughters stand on their own feet and have skills of their own.

It has been a long journey to this point in time. How we got here is part of the story of the Kenora Native Women's Association, which later became *Anishinaabe Kweg*. I am proud to have been part of this group that laid the path for our young women.

VIC

I was severely abused from the time my mother died until I was an adult. My attitude was, "I'll show you. I'll get back at you. I'll fight back." I was always trying to prove I was tougher than everyone else, but it just meant I was a human punching bag. When I met Vic my life changed. He gave me the courage to love.

I was twenty-nine years old and working at the Lake of the Woods Hotel when I met Vic. He was a smaller man, but I'm so short I still had to look up to him. He was very, very shy; I wasn't, so it was easier for him to be with me. He told me stories that interested me. Listening to him, I realized even though he had a rough life, he never hurt anyone.

He grew up with his mother in Winnipeg, Manitoba. They were very poor. He told me about going door-to-door selling donuts to get enough money to survive. During the Depression, he travelled coast to coast with other young men looking for whatever work they could find to survive. He served during the Second World War. There is a handsome picture of him in his uniform that I treasure. He would never speak about the war, though.

After his service, he returned to Winnipeg. When his mother died, he came to Kenora. He came here because it's where his nephew lived. Vic began working for a bush contractor and after awhile he started working on his own.

Contracts started coming in and he needed men to help him. He took his nephew's advice and began hiring. There were other good, hardworking men out on the streets that were wishing for jobs in tree planting and pulpwood cutting. These were my people. Vic was not *Anishinaabe*, but he treated them with respect. He hired them and they found hope in the work provided by my husband. The forestry department didn't give out spring and summer contracts at that time because of the risk of forest fires. But Vic found other work for his men during the off-season periods. He remembered his own hard times and cared about his workers. How he cared for my people caught my attention.

Vic had a cabin at Hilly Lake where he and his workers lived while they were contracting. One time when he was picking up staff, I decided I wanted to go too. I began helping out as I did with my father and uncles. I watched the men and I decided I wanted to do more.

Vic let me try whatever interested me. I knew he preferred I stick to de-limbing the trees after he chopped them down because it was safer, but he knew better than to try to tell me what to do. I loved him for that respect.

Our feelings grew as we worked together. Our respect was the foundation for how we came together. Without respect, relationships don't grow. He would listen to my opinion. If we didn't agree, we never fought. There was never a time when Vic tried to tell me what to do. He was a patient man who trusted me and allowed me to walk my own path. The more he encouraged me to be me, the more I loved him for who he was.

The chainsaws brought in to make life easier also made life harder. For contractors, it meant fewer workers could cut more wood. For workers, this meant they were laid off sooner as there was less work. The good men Vic had hired were employed less and less. With the loss of work, their self-respect also lessened. Some ended up on the streets of Kenora. First came the men who couldn't cut pulp anymore. Then came the next wave of men who could no longer work as guides because tourism declined. Now it is young people who have found their way to the streets because they have lost their self-respect.

If losing respect takes you to the streets, finding respect will take people off the street. *Nindede* said respect is the first law of our people. As a people we need to follow our own traditional laws because they developed out of the wisdom of our ancestors.

Vic and I eventually lived on the Jones Road. Vic had actually built that road with a horse and skidder. He was a hard worker. He never drank. I still went on a drunk from time to time, but the safer I felt with Vic, the less I felt the need. The need had risen from all the negatives in my past—anger over the abuse, the loss of my culture, the residential school experience. I used those negatives to go into the streets to drink. I didn't drink at our home. Our home was a positive place, and I kept it separate from my anger. When I would come back from a binge Vic just welcomed me back. He never judged me or resented my addiction. I couldn't understand why he didn't just kick me out. He loved me unconditionally, and this gave me hope. With time I stopped hurting myself with drink, and I found the courage to marry this wonderful man. He was a gift to me from the Creator.

After I had stopped drinking I became pregnant. Today, with what we have learned about fetal alcohol syndrome, I am very, very grateful I had not been drinking while pregnant. I am also glad I did not have children until I was grown up. I look around now and see babies having babies. It was not like this when I was young.

Vic and I cut a lot of pulp together. One day while we were out working in the woods, I gave him a worry—but it was a good worry. I told him that we were going to have a baby. He was shocked and then asked, "What will we feed a baby?" I laughed.

He was worried we would not have enough. He grew up poor, and he wanted to give much more to his children. When our daughter was born he spoiled her. Vic loved being a father, and was not so worried when I was expecting again. He was thrilled when our son was born. Even with two children there was always enough.

Family life did not keep us from wandering through the bush. We loved it too much. On Vic's days off we would pack up sandwiches and head back into the woods. He would put the baby in his packsack and off we would go. He would lead us into many areas, but always led us home. I would show him things I had learned as a young girl. I smoked meat and fish for the winter. I taught him to waste nothing. I showed him what clay to use for pottery. I showed him how to gently pick the wild rice by hand. The rice beds have since been harmed by White men with motorized boats that pulled up everything by the roots. Without roots there is no regrowth.

Vic was respectful of my knowledge. He helped me tan hides, find natural medicines and snare rabbits. I showed him, and I tried to interest my children. Unfortunately, children don't always recognize the gift you are trying to give them.

My biggest regret is I did not make sure they learned to speak our language. Their dad spoke English, as well as their friends and teachers. The children didn't feel like they needed more than that.

When the children were babies, I was at home more. I kept busy with crafts and other little house industries that made me a little money on the side. Vic supported us, but I was proud I could provide special treats for my family out of my own work. It kept my sense of independence.

Vic built our home on the Jones Road. It was good place, and the land holds many memories of our family times. Many types of trees surrounded us. Our garden drew in animals. Rabbits and squirrels and birds chased about. Deer and bears roamed by as they migrated through the woods. We also had pets—horses, ponies, dogs and cats. Our dog was a very good watchdog, and let us know when anyone, or any animal, came too close. Sometimes foxes would drop by. Our special visitors were the eagles that have a special role in our world. They bring us wisdom. White eagles are rare—and revered as spirit birds.

One day, my husband rose early to fire up the wood stove and make the coffee. This was his routine. Once the coffee was ready he would get me up to make breakfast. One morning, I smelled the coffee but he hadn't come to wake me yet. I went into the kitchen and saw him standing by the window looking out. Without turning he asked me if I had ever seen a big white bird that wasn't a sea gull. I looked and called our friend, who was staying with us, to come look. Between us, we recognized it was most like an eagle despite its colour.

I motioned my husband to follow me out. With tobacco in my hand, I spoke to the eagle. In the language of my people, I said, "Thank you for blessing us with your presence." The white eagle listened, and then turned west. The great bird spread its wings and flew up to the sky.

A visit from a white eagle is an honour and we had been blessed. The white eagle returned three more times. In keeping with our medicine wheel, four is a special number. To have four visits had great meaning for us.

The white eagle's final visit was to my daughter. It was a cold and rainy day, and she had come to the house to bring something for her dad. As she was leaving she noticed what she thought was a white bag flapping on a branch. When she walked toward the bag, it moved away. Startled she stood and watched. It turned to look at her and she realized it was the white eagle. This was the blessing's final visit.

Even though Vic was most comfortable in the bush, as a family we also travelled to show the children new places on our camping vacations. One year we went to Niagara Falls. Vic's sisters lived near there, in Oakville. Family was important to Vic, and he wanted our children to know all of his relatives. It was a good time but it was an adventure. Vic's shyness meant I had to be the guide, and I didn't know the area. I had to ask questions of everyone to make sure we were going in the right direction. The children loved living in a tent and seeing new things.

We also went to Banff four years later. We were headed to Shoal Lake, Manitoba, for a visit and then decided to keep on going. Vic had been to many of places we stopped. During his years on the road Vic had travelled coast-to-coast looking for work. He showed the children and I where he had been in those days and talked about the changes. My children still like to travel. They have been to many places Vic and I only heard about.

Vic was very good with the children. He was a humble man, and did not speak much, but he knew what was right and what was wrong. He spoiled the children, but he also made sure we taught them how to take care of themselves because we would not always be there for them. It was up to us to raise them with skills. It was very important to Vic that our children were educated so they could provide for their own families.

My daughter remembers how her father was always after her to brush her teeth. He would tell her it was easier to take care of her teeth now than to pay the dentist later. It was a lesson about being careful today so tomorrow would be better. Vic did not want his children to struggle as he had. He believed education was the way to success. My father also believed this, and my brothers went on to higher education. My bad experiences at the residential school meant I wanted no part of any school. I had to learn from life.

In December, we earned extra money by selling Christmas trees. Vic would set aside the tops of the trees he was cutting and we would sell them from our house. We became well-known for our nice trees. People would call us early in the season to make sure we saved one for them. The extra money helped Santa to visit generously. My children didn't have to make their own gifts as I did at residential school.

We lived a modest life but there was always enough. We even had some money put aside for when our son went to university. Our daughter went to college. We must have been good with money because both of our children are now working as financial advisors. They learned something from us.

My children were also hard workers. I remember our son working two jobs while he was still in high school in order to save money for university. He would finish up at his first job and walk across the street to work his second job. Vic would have to go to pick him up when he finished work at two o'clock in the morning. Later our son worked full-time and travelled to Winnipeg after his shift so he could complete his master's degree. Not many people would be willing to work and do their schooling at the same time. Our daughter was equally ambitious. She went to college while she still had young children at home. It was a challenge but she met it well. My children say they succeeded because of their parents. But I say they succeeded because of their own hard work.

When Vic's health began to fail, he could no longer go into the bush. This took the spirit out of him. When he went into the nursing home I moved into town to be closer to him. Every day I was able to walk over to spend time with him. It was precious time. He has left us now, but I believe I will see him soon enough in the Spirit World. Faith brings us through all things.

BECOMING A SOCIAL ACTIVIST

Work together and you will rise up together.

This is the teaching that is the key to healing our scarred and wounded past. I have seen how it works, and I will tell you how it worked for us.

Through my early years with Vic, I was moving towards sobriety. It took me about six years to straighten my path. People often ask me how I did it. It was hard—but it was also simple. I asked for spiritual help and guidance every day. I still live each day like that—one day at a time, and with the help of the Creator. My sobriety was a gift from the Creator. Having been given the gift, it is my responsibility to share it with others.

Not only had I changed, but the world around me was also changing. In 1965, over 400 *Anishinaabe* marched through Kenora in protest against the conditions we lived. Poverty had spread through our people with the destruction of our traditional ways. Without new resources for our communities there was no hope for any of us. Racism prevented us from eating in certain restaurants or obtaining jobs that might lift us from low-income, seasonal work. The effects of mercury poisoning physically disabled our people. Our self-respect had been destroyed through generations of colonization and residential school abuse.

My brother led the march along with other native leaders. I was scared because I didn't know what would happen. I didn't understand how walking down a street would change everything. But I've since learned that action makes change. Sometimes it's fast and sometimes it's slower, but doing something is better than doing nothing.

On the day of the march, many of our people were fearful. We had never done anything like this before. I stayed home with my children but I heard how it was. It was a mixture of anger and hope that pushed our people forward—moving through the town in a tsunami of brown faces. When it was done we were mostly relieved. No one was hurt. In walking, we had finally felt the power of our people again.

Later people told me this was the start of our civil rights movement in Canada. Journalists came and wrote about the conditions we lived with. As they spread our stories, others came. The Ontario Human Rights Commission formed a committee with indigenous leaders and the town council to talk together but talk alone didn't bring change.

This first civil rights march called for action. Each inch had to be fought—but I was a fighter. They couldn't stop us, but they did their best to discourage us. At best we were ignored. At worst we were vilified. The residential school system was finally shut down. Some people stepped forward who understood how racism and residential school had damaged us. Still, it was another forty years before the government accepted any accountability.

My children were born and began to grow up. Around 1969 I started dropping by the Fellowship Centre where I was made welcome. At that time the Centre was just a drop-in at a small house. My son was still a toddler, but my daughter had started school. Having been helped, I wanted to help others. At first people were suspicious of me because they remembered my past. Everyone knew me from my life on the streets, and they waited for me to fail.

Soon after my introduction to the Fellowship Centre a new building was constructed. I am always curious about new things so I started dropping by more often. Dropping in became volunteering. It felt good to help others, and I spent more and more time at the Centre. My husband was very supportive of this.

Many of our people stepped forward to reclaim our traditions. Meetings were held at the Waystation, which later became the Lake of the Woods Powwow Club. The Club's mission was to bring together, and it brought the strength of our past with the needs of our present. We worked together to teach young people our traditions. We healed through powwows and socials. We celebrated sobriety. Together we all became stronger and raised ourselves up together. Most importantly, we raised up the drum.

Chief Dan George taught me a very important lesson about helping my people. I was at a workshop in Brandon. I was attending with my children, and I arrived late into his session. I quickly began taking notes, trying to catch up. At the break, Chief George came to speak to my friend and I. We learned about how we should listen respectfully to people. He said:

> *"We are a people of oral tradition. When we take a pen and paper to write down what our people are saying, we seem like White social workers to them. Many social workers and government agents have come to our people with pen and paper. After they leave they take something with them. It was always about what they could take away with their paper.*
>
> *Our ancestors gave us the gift of listening. We need to use this gift. Our people stop talking from their hearts when they will think that you are not listening from your heart. Listening from the heart is a gift. If you listen this way, anything you hear will be remembered and anything you say will come from your heart.*

*When you speak from the heart it will go straight into
their hearts."*

The provincial Ministry of Community and Social Services
hired me to help with the homelessness problem. I don't know
what they thought I would do for them, but I know they didn't
like having things stirred up. But I only know one way to solve
problems, and that is to do something about it. I found out sometimes you get hired to keep the problems quiet. Problems are like
tears—they have to come out so you can release them.

HOMELESSNESS IN KENORA

In 1973, a very good friend of mine worked with me on the report "While People Sleep". For months we struggled to bring the hard truth of our lives forward. Within less than four years, nearly 200 Indians died violently in the Kenora area. Most of the sudden deaths were accidental, and most involved alcohol. In our effort to bring voices forward, we walked the back alleys where my people were huddled. I had once been there too. We trudged through the bush to find where our people were living in cardboard lean-tos because there was no place for them. We asked the questions no one ever asked before.

I will always remember the young woman we found on one of our searches. We had heard she was living in the woods where the Walmart parking lot is now. It was winter when we finally found her by following the smoke of her fire. Her only shelter was a windbreak she had build by nailing boards between trees and stretching plastic bags over the boards to keep out the wind. She was pregnant and had no place to go. Wild animals had better, warmer shelter than she did.

I went to social services to get help, but they just fired me because I made this young woman's problems public. It didn't matter. We took it upon ourselves to make a change for her without the government's help. Wauzhushk Onigum agreed to let us build a small cabin for her on their land. Volunteers brought supplies and built the tiny home. There was enough room for a bed and a stove to heat the one-room shelter. The women made quilts out of old clothing. There was no water or electricity, but many of us didn't have those anyways. We moved the young woman in before her daughter was born. Sadly, Children's Aid took the baby and the young mother lost her heart. Like so many others she turned to drink to blot out the pain.

My friend took my people's words and researched the facts that supported what they told us. The report, While People Sleep, was stark and powerful for anyone who cared to read it. The recommendations were respectful and specific. The Kenora Social Planning Council and Treaty 3 brought the report forward. Thirty years later some of those recommendations have been implemented. Other recommendations were implemented and then abandoned as political priorities changed. The rest still sit on a shelf in the book.

After further activism in the community, funding came through for the NeChee Friendship Centre and the street patrol. We began to plan for ourselves in the community. It was an exciting time. There were efforts to discourage us, but they could not stop us. We felt very alone against the townspeople. However, as time went on, other caring people in the community came forward to show their respect and support for our efforts.

At the Fellowship Centre we were given the downstairs space to develop programs. We didn't know anything about programming, funding or administration, but we did it anyways. I was not the only one. Community leaders and town people helped us to make things happen. My heart is full of the memories of these special people.

I started making soup, and others joined me. Soon we were doing many things—rummage sales, sewing circles, cribbage. The women wanted to do more. I noticed people jumping in to help with our projects. There were many volunteers, including those who had been on the streets themselves. That's what helps get people sober—having something to do that makes them feel good and useful.

There are many good memories of this time. Music also served us well. Some of our regular volunteers were talented and often performed for our pleasure. One fellow came up with the idea to have a danceathon as a fundraiser for the youth. With the director's permission, we organized chaperones, music and food. It was great fun and everyone had a good time while raising money for the Centre.

WOMEN HELPING WOMEN

I was offered a job with Treaty 3 as a community development worker, which allowed me to be paid for what I was doing already. Unfortunately, meetings seemed to take up most of my time, and I missed the work at the Fellowship Centre. A staff member from the Indian Community Branch called me one day to talk. She and her co-workers thought we should apply to fund a project to help our women become gainfully employed. We all knew how important having paid employment was to our people. Without jobs we would never become independent again since we couldn't live off the land anymore.

We formed the Kenora Native Women's Association. Women from outside of town came in to join our association, so our membership grew. Our ties were strengthened by the women's conferences we held. Older women brought their experience. Barrier busters gave us reason to believe all things were possible. Younger women came forward with their enthusiasm and hopefulness. We met to talk, and in our sharing we recognized our common goals as *Anishinaabe* women.

The first project of our association was a plan to help aboriginal women find work to support them and their families. The Indian Community Branch helped us to write the proposal for Ki Kaa Wee Chi'een (I'll Help You). There was so much I had to learn about proposal submissions, incorporations and project management. Our first proposal was not accepted, but we were encouraged to continue trying.

Finally a six-month trial was approved. We were required to hire six women and place them in real jobs. The hospital was the first to receive one of our workers. She was to be an interpreter and service guide for *Anishinaabe* patients. Following this, other partnering organizations offered potential placements, including the jail, street patrol workers, courthouse, and both local nursing homes.

Support was provided for the placements. Many of us had limited education, so report writing was a challenge. We helped each other with spelling and other skills. We also needed to understand the systems around us—policing, courts, and social services. There was much to learn, but we never forgot our roots. Elders helped us to deal with the pressure of these challenges. We also had committed volunteers who helped us to develop.

The project grew and I was invited to speak about it at an out of town conference. Four out of our seven placements completed the program. The women felt they gained much through Ki Kaa Wee Chi'een. They came in believing they would not ever be hired for good jobs, but they took the challenge and found the determination to move forward in life. I was happy to let others know it was possible to create our own future through programs like ours. At the conference, I met a respected Elder who later visited us to share his own wisdom.

His story about thanking people, and honouring those who help, follows:

> *"There is an unwritten law that we do not count or list people. This was taught to us by Elders who have since left us to go to the Spirit World. We honour them by respecting this law.*
>
> *When people have helped us on a project it is important to remember and thank them in our thoughts as well as*

*in person. This is because they are individual people to
be honoured."*

I cannot count or list all of those who have helped, but I honour
them and my heart holds them close.

The Kenora Native Women's Association continued on through
Anishinaabe Kweg. We began by helping women to support each
other. Then we helped women get jobs. After that we went on to
help the youth through teaching and childcare. Whatever the need
was we worked together to make it happen.

WISDOM OF THE ELDERS

I learned many important lessons through my work with the Kenora Native Women's Association, but there is one crucial message that came to me through the experience.

During the project, volunteers came by to offer help and support. Some of these volunteers were living on the streets themselves, but they still came to help others. The Elders helped us to learn our past, to be encouraged in our present, and to reach for our future. The Fellowship Centre staff shared their space and expertise with us. We were not alone. We succeeded by working and reaching out to each other. My advice to all is: Work together. I spent many years pushing people away because of my anger. It was only when I reached out to others that success came.

The Fellowship Centre was a place where we could gather and share each other's company while doing meaningful work. There were always pots of tea and plates of fresh bannock available. Many program plans were developed during the endless games of cribbage played daily. It was a safe place for our people. Yet, even there we did not speak of our residential school experiences. Now I wonder why we all buried it so deep. All of us had suffered but none of us spoke.

My friend, Dr. Allan Torrie, kept poking at my own experiences like a man with a stick poking at a bear. He was a brave man to risk poking me. I would brush him away until one day I did finally speak. The words spilled out, as did the tears. I related experience after experience. As my story was told, the doctor patiently waited for me to finish. Finally, when I was drained of all words, he spoke. He put his own understanding to my experiences. I had been a young girl, living in an abusive environment. The abuse had been emotional, psychological and physical. Somehow I believed everything done to me had been the abuser's right, and I had no rights of my own.

I had turned the anger inside where it fed my addiction. To know that calling me a stupid, dirty Indian was emotional abuse made me realize those words were weapons. They were not descriptions of who I was. To understand that running costumed devils through our darkened halls to frighten us into Christianity was psychological abuse helped me to know the extent of the harm done to us all. To realize the priests and nuns did not have the right to beat us, made me accept they were doing wrong—not me. Do I hate them? No, but I remember, and call them to account for their abuses against children. I call the government to account for allowing this system to exist. I also call my people together to share their experiences and to begin healing. We must heal to move forward.

Dr. Torrie and his wife helped bring our traditional healing practices into the mainstream. He was a mentor to many of us. He helped me to understand how my past was creating so much anger in me, but he also understood the power of our traditional healing practices. It was taking back the traditions of my grandmother that returned me back to who I was before the abuse. This is why I regret having rejecting her teachings earlier, after the nuns had told me she was a witch. I could have learned so much more. So many of us have lost that knowledge. Those of us who have it must pass it on to our youth for their own healing.

Knowledge is a gift given to you that must be shared or it has no value. My cousin who worked on a local healing program shared his learning and eventually ran the Native Healers' program at the hospital.

My doctor friend encouraged me to work with the *Mishomis/ Nokomis* (Grandfather/Grandmother) project. The coordinator was worried because I have a reputation for disagreeing all the time. He finally came to understand it wasn't that I disagreed; it was that I was presenting an alternative to consider. My husband had recently had major surgery, and I did not want to travel too much. They promised me I could stay close to my husband during his recovery. We got funding for four years.

We began holding Elders' Gatherings. Our people came together to learn from each other, to share our traditional wisdom, and to plan for future generations. Once our group was established we dared to begin speaking of our pain. The legacy of residential school abuse affected us all—generation after generation. Hurt piled onto hurt until we all were wounded. We needed the strength of the Elders to guide us forward.

With its success, the project was extended for another eight years. When the program ran out of funding, I wanted to continue the work, so I kept doing it. I'm still doing the work started in that time. I get tired but I'm still going. I have the trust of the street people. I have the respect of the community.

I took part in the government's Truth and Reconciliation Hearings. It was an awful experience. I tried to tell my story but they gave us time limits. You can't limit your pain to a schedule. I felt pushed into someone else's process. It wasn't about me any more. If there is no time to tell your full truth, then you haven't been fully heard.

I had also volunteered to help with the healing after the sessions. I struggled to not get caught up in the pain that surrounded me as I worked with the survivors. When it was over, I needed air. I walked home but I didn't make it. The spirit went out of me and I crumpled up inside. I fell into the snowbank and sat there feeling empty inside. I realized then I also had to take time to heal. I am more careful now.

I continued to hold healing workshops at the Fellowship Centre. The drummers welcomed the survivors and it become a time of sharing for us that respects who are. We told the stories of experiences that hurt us and then danced together in unity. The final song was always a healing song to send us travelling on our own paths.

In 2006, I joined with other Kenora residents to start a new movement—Making Kenora Home. It is new, but it is also old. In 1973, my brother, Tobasonakwat Kinew, told council, "Kenora is our home and we have a right to live comfortably in this town." Thirty-five years later, Making Kenora Home issued their guiding principles, which begin with the acknowledgement, "Our community has experienced many hurts in the past and we are committed to moving forward toward our vision of a more caring and mutually respectful community."

Respect for all people living in Kenora guided the writing of the "While People Sleep" report. We saw the need for proper housing. Without housing, there is no hope. Making Kenora Home took up the call for the right to adequate, accessible and affordable housing for all who live in our community.

There is always work to be done—residential school recovery, environmental issues, and homelessness. It all interests me and there is always something to learn, something to teach, something I can do to make the future better for my grandchildren, my great-grandchildren, and all my relations. We are all related, and a better future for some, is a better future for all.

Workshops energize me. The Creator is always invited to join us. Together we work through our emotions and from the gathering the Creator will take our hopes and dreams. We may not understand how it will be handled, and it might not be in the time that we want, but the Creator's time and plan is bigger than our understanding. Together we cry, and then we laugh, because good comes out of our tears. We exist to boost each other up. There has been so much negative, but there is also positive in our world. Enjoy it.

TRUTH & RECONCILIATION:
RESPONDING TO GENOCIDE

Our grandmothers and grandfathers taught us to forgive because holding anger hurts us. It is hard to talk about forgiveness in a land strewn with the aftermath of a cultural genocide. As I walk down the street I see the people who have lost their dignity to addictions. I speak with families that have been torn apart by the alienation created by residential schools. I hold the hands of victims of sexual violence. I sit beside the bodies of those whose release from the pain of their dislocated lives was caused by self-harm.

By trying to kill the Indian within each of us, unfathomable intergenerational pain was inflicted. Survivors struggle with the effects of childhood abuse that included physical, emotional and psychological trauma. The results are addictions, unemployment, family breakdown, violence, and hopelessness.

Our Elders tell us it is forgiveness that leads us back to life. At a Truth and Reconciliation Hearing, I listened to the apologies. I thought of my grandmother's lessons and then I spoke: "I was taught to forgive but no one has taught me how to forget."

This is our reality as survivors. Sometimes the pain abates, but memories come back and we struggle again to reconcile ourselves to the pain. This is the truth. Our future lies in our past. We will move forward as we regain control of our destiny through our own language, our own culture, and our own teachings. With this return to the past, we will regain our identity and will move forward in dignity as we were meant to live.

I am a woman of hope and I believe that together, and with the Creator's help, we can go into a better place. But change only happens when action follows talk.

The Truth and Reconciliation Commission has brought the issues of my people forward for public discussion—but talk is cheap. We tell you what was done and how it affected us. We look at each other and then our meeting is over. Healing is a long process, and it is different for each and every one of us. I had a grandmother who raised me with love. This helped make residential school more bearable. I had a man who loved me until I found my way. Not everyone has, or had, those things. It will take longer for others who have been damaged in far greater ways. They will get up and stumble but with help they will get up yet again.

When the Commission began its work, money flowed to help these people. The Commission opened up the wounds. This is a good thing when someone is there to tend to the person whose hurt is flowing. I, myself, worked for several of the projects set up to teach our people what the schools had stolen from them. Now the speeches are done, and the money is no longer there. Projects are cancelled even though the people can tell you how helpful they have been. Our people are worse off than they were to start. Emotions have been stirred up. Help was offered and then snatched away because my people did not heal fast enough to meet the government's schedule.

We need continued support to heal in our own time. We need resources to help our most hurt people to begin living in a positive way. We know how residential school pain is often disguised by addictions, and then the addiction prevents recovery. We know many of the people who were most affected are now living on the streets because no one wants them. There are no affordable rental units available, and if they are available landlords won't rent to to a high-risk tenant.

We need to wrap our victims up in a blanket of caring—put a roof over their head, food on their tables, and mentors to support them when they lose their balance. We need to care enough not to limit our help to meetings or schedules. These survivors are whole people. We cannot treat just parts of them. That is core to our beliefs. Healing is holistic.

TEACHINGS

Teachings, by oral or singing traditions, have been handed down from generation to generation, both by Elders and teaching lodges. Elders have many messages to offer including spiritual knowledge, legends, prophecies and history. Respect for our Elders, healers and teachers should always be foremost in our daily lives so our people can continue to practice our traditional gifts.

The residential school system stole this knowledge. Our culture and language were destroyed. When you destroy a person's identity, you destroy the person. In trying to kill the Indian inside us, they hollowed us out. Without heart and spirit, we lost our self-respect.

The path back to wholeness is to reclaim the wisdom of our ancestors. We need the living language that vividly shared the traditions that kept us strong in the past. We need to honour these traditions through practice. We need to teach and share the gifts the Creator gave our people. It is not too late.

Seven Fires Story

Seven Anishinaabe *youths were walking together. Like most youth they were looking for something to do. They encountered a man sitting by his dwelling place. The man invited them to sit with him so he could share a prophecy with them.*

The Elder told the youth they had been chosen to represent the Anishinaabe *nations in a sacred quest to gather prophecies from across the land. Their journeys would lead them to places they never saw before and they met many people with different tribes and different languages. Through the stories offered to them by Elders, the future was unfolded. The* Anishinaabe *would emerge through seven fires—each marking an era of change for the people.*

First Fire

The people will follow the Sacred Shell held by the Medewewin *Lodge to where their new home will be. It is a long path, and there will be seven stopping places along the way. The strength of* Medewewin *will be the strength of the people.*

Second Fire

At the second stopping place, the people will lose the Sacred Shell. The Medewewin *will weaken, but a boy will bring the people back to the traditional ways. These are the stepping-stones to the future* Anishinaabe.

Third Fire

The Anishinaabe *will find their way to a land in the West where the food grows upon the waters. This will be their land.*

Fourth Fire

A light-skinned race will come. They will bring friendship and knowledge through a handshake. If they come with respect, shared knowledge will bring a wonderful change for generations. If these people come with weapons, they will be filled with greed. Our best lands will be taken. The rivers will run with poison and the fish will not be fit to eat.

Fifth Fire

There will be a time of great struggle for all native people. Someone will come promising great salvation and people will abandon the old teachings. The new way is a false promise, and the people will nearly be destroyed by it.

Sixth Fire

Life will become filled with grief. Grandsons and granddaughters will turn against the Elders, and the Elders will lose their purpose in life. A new sickness will come and the people will become unbalanced.

Seventh Fire

A new people will emerge. They will retrace their steps to find what was lost. They will ask Elders to guide them, but many of the Elders will not speak because they have nothing to say. They have fallen asleep. If the new people can rebirth the Anishinaabe *Nation through the drum of the* Medewewin *Lodge, the Sacred Fire will be lit again. The light-skinned race will have a choice; if they chose respect, catastrophe will be avoided.*

Eighth Fire

If the right choice has been made, the Seventh Fire will light the final fire. This will be a time of peace, love and respect where all will live together in wisdom.

It is the responsibilities of the Elders to teach each generation about the Seven Fires. Without knowledge of the Seven Fires, the Eighth Fire will never be lit. I often had reservations about reciting the disturbing stories I was told because I did not want to believe in their truth. But, as I grew into an Elder myself, the stories became something I could feel. I knew they were warnings. We have to carry these warnings to all of the people.

THE FOUR DIRECTIONS

Within a medicine wheel there are many teachings. The Four Directions keep us balanced as humans.

The East Quadrant (*waabuning*) is our beginning, as is spring and morning. When we are born, we leave the Spirit World and enter the physical world. We must honour the gift of life through tobacco. Life always moves clockwise and so does our journey through the Four Directions.

The next quadrant is the South (*zhaawanong*), which is a time for youthful vigour and searching for spiritual growth. To live well during summer growth, we must cultivate and nurture our youth so their spirits grow strong. Cedar cleanses and heals us during this turbulent time.

The West (*paangizhmook*), where the sun goes down, is the adult stage. As adults we need to sift all matters through our hearts—evaluating and moving forward with compassion for others. Sage clears our minds and hearts for our adult responsibilities in the community.

As we age we move toward the North *(kiiwedinong)*. It is a time of rest and remembrance—creating the wisdom of the Elders. The teachings of the Elders can guide us through our lives as sweetly as the sweet grass.

WATER

Women were given the responsibility for water. As a water carrier, the sacredness of water is a special concern to me. I have lived long enough to see the poisoning of the Wabigoon-English River System and the impact upon the peoples who fished these waters. I have seen the blue algae spreading through our lakes. I protested the shutdown of the Environmental Lakes research facility that was our only hope to redeem our waters. Now is the time to make the right choices—later will be too late.

OVERCOMING BAD MEMORIES

Do not look back at the past—especially when sorrow has been experienced. Remembering pain feeds hurt, anger and hatred. These emotions latch onto us, causing destruction. Help is needed to free us from the corrosion of these three dangers.

Instead of looking back, look ahead and dream—envisioning a better future. Use the Elders' wisdom to move forward into that better place. It is there for our benefit. All we have to do is ask for help.

POVERTY

The idea of poverty came with the White settlers. They looked at us, and because we did not have what they had, they believed we were impoverished. We were not. We always had food to nourish us, clothing to cover us, and shelter from the weather. Because our food, clothing and shelter were different, they thought we were without.

We did not carry much with us because we were nomadic. Things that were not useful to us did not matter as we travelled. We followed the food the Creator provided. We knew how to use the gifts well. Our Elders taught us how to harvest and preserve the foods for our future use. Each season brought a new bounty, and we were grateful.

Our clothing served a purpose. It kept us warm and dry. We even had our own fashions that reflected our sense of natural beauty. Our shelter forms were dry in the summer and warm in the winter. Our tipis packed up and travelled well as we travelled over Mother Earth .

We did not consider ourselves poor. We were more often called upon to help the Whites survive when they lost their own supplies. They did not know how to live in our world. We were rich in our own world.

DREAM CATCHERS

Sacred dream catchers (*bawaajege naagwaagunun*) were often hung above small children as a protection. The wooden frames hold a spider's web that catches bad dreams. Good dreams pass through and slide down the soft feathers to the sleeping child.

To make a *bawaajege naagwaagun* dig around the roots of a birch or willow tree. Find a root about a quarter-inch thick and cut it from the tree. Using a root preserves the tree. One root can make about four small dream catchers. Shape the root piece by soaking and tying it into a round shape. Traditionally, sinew was used to weave the web around the frame, but people started to use yarn and decorative beads when they became available. Finally, feathers are tied to the amulet to allow the dreams to slide down softly to the baby. A real *bawaajege naagwaagun* is smudged, so it must be respected as blessed.

SMUDGING

Combinations of the four sacred plants are used to help purify and cleanse sacred items and us. As with all things, smudging works best in a circle that mimics the cycle of life.

A small amount of tobacco, sweet grass, sage and cedar are put into a shell or bowl to be lit for the smudge. The smoke is directed with a feather or fan toward the people, area or items being purified while the smudge pot is walked slowly in a clockwise circle. People who are being smudged can help bring the smoke toward them for cleansing. Typically, people will draw the smoke to their heart, their head, their arms, and downwards to their legs. Smudging helps to centre us and can be done as often as wanted.

ASKING FOR AN ELDERS HELP

Tobacco (*aasamah*) is given in respect to an Elder if you are seeking their help. When the healer accepts the tobacco it means they are ready to hear your request. The Elder will take the tobacco and either put some of it into a pipe for burning or will go to place some in a clean place (usually under a tree). When the Elder offers the gifted tobacco, they will say a prayer. Prayer prepares the Elder to help you.

The Elder may give instructions immediately to the person seeking advice, or they may need to make arrangements to obtain medicines or plan a ceremony. It is very important the person requesting help remains respectful and patient.

SEVEN GRANDFATHER TEACHINGS

The teachings of honesty, humility, courage, wisdom, love, generosity, and most importantly, respect are gifts to our people. Living the teachings makes you a gift. Without respect you cannot attain any of the other qualities.

When I was young I did not have respect myself. I told the truth, but I hid the abuse of residential schools. I did not have the confidence to be humble because I did not respect myself. I was tough but I did not have real courage. I knew things but believed I knew more than I did. I made love but I did not love. I shared some of what I had but I didn't give with a grateful heart. Respecting myself, respecting others, respecting our culture, and respecting Mother Earth brought me closer to the teachings.

ANGER

If someone is angry with you, don't get angry with him or her. You must just stay still and listen to their angry words. They'll get tired and start to wonder what's wrong with you that you don't want to fight. There is no need to take their anger on to you. It's their own burden, not yours. Eventually when you see them again, they may be friendly, and you can become friends.

WALKING YOUR PATH

Walk slowly through the Earth, learning as you go, and be humbled with the realization you can be a better person.

OUR LAWS

The *Anishinaabe* people have laws that must be respected and observed. These laws ensure we do not hurt Mother Earth or our brothers and sisters. In this world we are all brothers and sisters who are dependent on Mother Earth for our sustenance.

CIRCLE OF ENERGY

The power to change us can be found in the energy of the
Circle. Within the Circle is the truth of our lives. That truth sup-
ports us in moving toward a good life. We enter the Circle when
we acknowledge the pain of the past, the reality of now, and the
hope of the future. Denying our past disables our spirit. Denying
today's reality creates delusions. Denying tomorrow's hope puts us
into fearfulness. The Circle has always existed and will continue to
be there for our support as long as the sun shines.

PONDS AND RIPPLES

Everyone has a purpose for being here on Mother Earth. We
have choices and are capable of taking action. We can learn. We can
share our knowledge with each other—and with the generations
to come.

Truth shapes our lives and it is our responsibility to live the
truth. We can learn that truth from each other, from observing
those around us, and from nature.

When you see a small pool of water—stop. Pick up a pebble
and throw it to the middle of the pond. The rock will sink, but if
you watch, ripples are created. Those ripples spread out in their
journey to the shore. Sometimes a breeze will interrupt the flow,
but the ripple adjusts and continues its path. Remember this when
you feel like you are sinking in life. We may disappear under the
water but our life force will continue to ripple to the end.

EAGLES

Eagles soar between our world and the Creator. They can see
the past, present and future. Our people believe eagles are the
special messengers that bring courage and wisdom. Their feathers

are sacred because of the teaching within them and are often used during ceremonies.

The dropping of an eagle feather requires careful handling. If dropped during a ceremony, or in a powwow, the ceremony is stopped immediately. The feather is retrieved from the ground and a decision must be made as to where the feather should be handed. Sometimes it is returned to the one who dropped it. Sometimes it is given to another. When the decision is made, the Elder sprinkles the ground where it fell with tobacco and says a prayer. With the help of the drum, an honour song is raised, and the feather is given to the chosen recipient.

BEAVERS

Elders teach us to learn from the animals around us. The beaver was given two important gifts that create wisdom for survival. These gifts are determination and patience.

Beavers need to build their dams to survive. First, they build their homes to stay dry. If the dam breaks, they build it again. They don't rest yet because winter is coming. Beavers busily gather supplies for their future needs. They work with patience toward their goal, and with determination to rebuild and restore when needed. People can learn from this example. When you lose what you have—begin again, without complaining. When you are tired, push forward until the tasks are completed. Reaching any goal requires determination and patience. Our ancestors understood the lesson of the beavers.

CLANS

My *nookum* made sure I knew my clan. She told me I had to know where I belonged. But, because we were punished for our traditional knowledge, I avoided even thinking about it. This knowledge stayed in the back of mind until I returned to the ways of our ancestors. Knowing our clans helps us to know what our purpose is within Creation. There are now many, many clans. Each clan had an identity in the community. I am Lynx Clan and we walk the land protecting our people. We know the land and we have learned about the natural medicines that can be used to treat illnesses. There were also rules about marriage between clans.

SACRED TRUTHS

We all have a purpose for being on Mother Earth (Ogashiinan). In the Spirit World, we can search for those reasons and lessons that help us make good choices in our lives.

Everything happens for a reason. Every crisis, sickness and conflict has a lesson for us within it.

Life is constantly changing and this is our opportunity to rebuild. We all make mistakes but when we realize that—when we admit our mistakes and ask forgiveness—we start anew.

We live our lives in seasons. The spring is our youth and is a time of budding growth. We bloom in the summer into adulthood. During the fall, we harvest and feast on the gifts of our lives. Winter brings us storytelling, teaching and rest. Each season has its own blessing and should be enjoyed in its own time.

Living justice does exist. Everything we do comes round the circle and returns to us, so we must be kind.

Everything in Creation is interconnected and mutually dependent. Every rock, tree, plant, bird and animal has a spirit and is part of our living Earth. We must respect that spirit and teach our young to protect our world.

Everyone has free will. As parents, we can guide, teach, and be real examples of good living for our youth. But, we cannot interfere with their chosen paths. To understand their paths, we must take the time to listen to them. To support them on their journey, we must walk beside them.

MEDICINES

There are four sacred plants, which are especially revered amongst the *Anishinaabe*. Each is associated with one of the Four Directions, and each has ceremonial and practical purposes that must be respected. Whenever a plant is picked, you must do it with respect. Pray to the plant, explaining why it is being picked and how it will help by becoming medicine. Always offer some tobacco in return for the plant's generosity in sharing itself so freely.

Tobacco (Aasamah)

The *Anicinaabe* came from the East and carried tobacco with them. It is used for communication and creating knowledge between people. *Aasamah* is a gift from the Creator (*Gizhe-manidoo*) and our people honour and respect this first medicine that came from Mother Earth. It is offered to the fire, to the drum, on clean ground, in a tree, or to an Elder.

When we pick it, we pray to *Gizhe-manidoo* to explain why we need it and to give thanks for it. To offer it, the tobacco is held in the left hand because it is closer to the heart. It is offered when seeking advice, when honouring the drum or pipe, or as a prayer to *Gizhe-manidoo*. Sometimes it is burnt and sometimes it is left to return to Mother Earth.

An offering of *aasamah* should be accepted as a show of honour. With the taking of the tobacco, the recipient takes on the responsibility for the task being asked. It is a sacred trust. The recipient then goes to a clean place in the forest to say a prayer for guidance.

The tobacco used today is no longer pure. It is often grown with harmful chemicals that enter your body causing cancer, respiratory sicknesses and heart disease. Since it is no longer pure, it is losing its power, as was foretold by our ancestors.

Cedar (Giizh-Kaandaag)

From the South, comes the cedar. The pine-scented branches of the cedar are separated into smaller pieces to be used in many ways. It can be dried and burnt for smudging. It can be boiled into a tea-like medicine called *mushkiki* which is good for colds and other respiratory problems. Sometimes *mushkiki* is used to ease stomach cramps, particularly during a woman's moon time.

Cedar can be made into a protection that blesses your home. To make this amulet, tie four branches together with string or yarn. Wrap a bit of tobacco in red or green cloth and attach it to the cedar. Hang the amulet above the door to ward off bad things. If it is put into your shoes, goodness will accompany you on your journey.

Sage (Maazhodewaashk)

This plant represents the western direction because that is where it comes from. It has a spicy scent and is used in much the same way as *giizh-kaandaag*. *Maazhodewaashk* purifies when it is burnt. It is often burnt to smudge the drum. Once the drum is smudged, the singers, offerings, food, and people are smudged.

Sweet Grass (Wiingaashk)

This plant has a beautiful aroma, and represents the northern direction of the medicine wheel. It is also a purifier. Usually people will braid cut sweet grass to keep it from drying out. The braid represents the hair of Mother Earth, and each section of the braid represents a sacred part of us—mind, body, and spirit. Like the braid, each part must be kept in balance so that we can be one.

To purify with a sweet grass braid, light one end. Let the smoke pass around you from head to foot. It is also good to keep wiingaashk in your vehicle.

PROPHECY

From the Elders I have learned about the hard times that would come to our people. I was a child when I heard these stories and now I am a great-grandmother.

It was foretold that the *Anishinaabe* would lose their respect, values and culture. Great sorrow and suffering would come out of this loss.

Strange sicknesses would strike down the people and the animals alike. I am seeing the devastation of cancers, sexually-transmitted diseases and blastomycosis.

The powerful medicines that were put on this Earth to heal us will lose their effectiveness. The animals will become unfit for eating. A trapper brought my husband a beaver he caught. It had blister-like sores on its flesh so could not be eaten.

The Elders told me even the water would become polluted and would make our people sick. The sickness will be hard to heal. I have lived to see mercury poisoning destroy the neurological systems of some of my people along the English and Wabigoon Rivers.

The animals, plants and water given to our people for their survival will be lost. Without these gifts, our people will forget how to support themselves. The destruction of our traditional way of life will darken their minds, and they will poison themselves with fire-water (alcohol) and strange medicines (drugs).

Tragedies will fall upon them. I look around and feel the pain of my people. There does not seem to be any healing between tragedies. We go from one grief to another.

The Elders promised there would come a time when my people would wake from their nightmare. They will see what is happening, and will learn they created these tragedies for themselves. When the people start to realize they have been dwelling in a dark cloud for far too long, they will ask for spiritual help.

The Creator will answer and the cloud will go away. People will mend their ways. The Seventh Generation will finally rise to help the people become strong. They will teach the young generation to follow the sacred teachings of our forefathers. I believe in the Elders' promise of the Seventh Generation.

STILL IN THE WORLD

The tiny figure is wrapped well against the winter. Each step, aided by her walker, is determined and steady. She moves toward her goal—a visit to a friend to talk about the business of the day, and perhaps a bit of chatting about yesterday.

She has an ongoing list of interests that require checking in at various offices around town. In between she speaks with her people. They converge on her from street corners and curb side. Sometimes they bring her news from the streets. Sometimes she brings them news from their families. It's called moccasin telegraph, and locals can attest to the speed of this non-electronic information dispersal.

Reaching her destination, she enters, and announces her arrival. Taken into the office, she parks her walker and seats herself. She takes off her layers—first removing the striped scarf that wraps around her neck. There is a bit of a struggle with the zipper but the thick parka eventually is draped open. A bright pink jogging jacket is revealed with a matching shirt peeking out at the edges. She tidies this inner layer and straightens up to begin her visit.

Her face shines like a burnished chestnut under the cuff of her toque. The toque is embellished with a knitted flower that droops down towards the coal dark eyes that dart around the room as she launches into her recitation of business. What is going on? What is being done? Who will help my people? Her questions come sharply.

In eighty-five years, her interest in the world around her has never waned. Curiosity drives her forward. Commitment keeps her active.

Business done, personal matters can be brought to the visit. She looks up at the ceiling, which is usually precursor to an interesting revelation. Mischief tugs at the corners of her mouth as she struggles to tell her story with modest dignity. She has never quite injected the expected sedateness that usually comes with age into her behaviours.

"When my father took me across the lake in the winter time, we had a sled and horses. It's different now." She waves away the memory and leans forward. "There are a lot of these snow machines now."

Dignity is overtaken by gleefulness, and her words tumble out. "I've done it myself, you know?"

"Driven a sled?" the host asks.

"A snow machine!" she blurts out. "At my age!"

The story spills out.

"I was visiting my daughter. They were driving snow machines. I was watching them going back and forth across the lake." Her hands illustrate the path of the machines. "I told them that it looked interesting, and they asked if I wanted to try it. I said, 'yes' fast—and then, I went!"

She settles back into the chair to share the experience.

"My children were not so happy. My son said I would probably go skydiving next!". She covers her mouth to stifle her soft chuckle. "I dressed up warm and was helped onto the seat. I sat there and they took me for a ride. It felt fast, but probably wasn't as fast as they sometimes go. Snow was flying as we moved across the lake. When we returned, we went back into the house, and that was it."

With chagrin replacing the chuckling, she admits, "Afterwards I was a bit sore but it was worth it. There are still new things in the world to try—and I'm still in this world".

ABOUT THE AUTHOR

As an ailing infant, Nancy was given her spirit name, Pay Comikeezhegook, and a prophecy. Fulfilling that promise, she became an advocate for her people. Her interests are broad- homelessness, addictions, reconciliation and healing. As a woman she fights fiercely against the victimization of aboriginal women and for environmental preservation. As a mother, grandmother and great-grandmother, she nurtures and heals those around her. As an elder she teaches the skills and wisdom of her ancestors to a new generation. Her work has been honoured by community activists, by the aboriginal people and by various governmental sectors. At 85 years of age, she lives each day with purpose, ceremony and commitment to the Creator.

Printed in Canada